MACRAMÉ FOR BEGINNERS

Decorate your Home and Garden with Creative Handmade Macramè Objects. A Complete Step-by-Step Guide to Projects, Knots, Patterns and much more.

BY JADE PAPER

© Copyright 2020 by Jade Paper - All rights reserved.

The content contained within this book may not be reproduced, duplicated or transmitted without direct written permission from the author or the publisher. Under no circumstances will any blame or legal responsibility be held against the publisher, or author, for any damages, reparation, or monetary loss due to the information contained within this book. Either directly or indirectly.

Legal Notice:

This book is copyright protected. This book is only for personal use. You cannot amend, distribute, sell, use, quote or paraphrase any part, or the content within this book, without the consent of the author or publisher.

Disclaimer Notice:

Please note the information contained within this document is for educational and entertainment purposes only. All effort has been executed to present accurate, up to date, and reliable, complete information. No warranties of any kind are declared or implied. Readers acknowledge that the author is not engaging in the rendering of legal, financial, medical or professional advice. The content within this book has been derived from various sources. Please consult a licensed professional before attempting any techniques outlined in this book.

By reading this document, the reader agrees that under no circumstances is the author responsible for any losses, direct or indirect, which are incurred as a result of the use of information contained within this document, including, but not limited to, — errors, omissions, or inaccuracies.

TABLE OF CONTENTS

Introduction 6

Chapter 1: What Is Macramé? 8

Chapter 2: Tools And Materials 16

Chapter 3: Types Of Macramé (Knots, Tricks, Cords) 24

Chapter 4: Other Knots 44

Chapter 5: Things To Look For In Choosing A Macramé Cord 54

Chapter 6: Macramé Plant Hangers 60

Chapter 7: Wall Hangings 74

Chapter 8: Macramé Bracelet 80

Chapter 9: Macramé Jewelry 88

Chapter 10: Indoor Project Ideas 110

Chapter 11:. Macramé Candle Holder 124

Chapter 12: How To Make Your Own Macramé Designs 134

Conclusion 148

Introduction

Taking a typical everyday space is the vision of most homeowners, and turning it into a space that will amaze visitors. The use of art made of macramé knots is a perfect way to make this dream come true. The art you put in your house should tell all about yourself and your personality. With so many artwork options made with macramé ties, there's no doubt you will find anything that fits your personality and style. The best thing is that all these artworks are handmade, so they are all one-of-a-kind creations, and will definitely delight your visitor the next time they enter your home.

These pieces of art can be found online, and whoever can tie knots can also make them. Now I know that most of you think of the macramé your grandmothers used to make. I know that if I think about macramé, the first thing that comes to my mind is the plant hangers from the early '80s of the late '70s. It's not difficult to find items made with macramé knots to match with any decor you have in your house with the range of materials used. These pieces of art can then be placed in your home, particularly any room with nautical decor, to add some special touches.

Decorations that can accentuate any shelf, wall, or bar are good to have. Wouldn't a Rum bottle decorated with macramé knots look 100 times better than the same old, drab bottle sitting in a bar or shelf? Imagine pouring a drink from a rope-covered bottle for a friend, then handing them their drink to put on a coaster made of rope, all this after they came into your house and also rubbed their feet on your rope-covered floor mat. Finally, a home decor that is really one of a kind, and now, instead of the other way around, the Jones will keep to you. What we all want is a space with a lovely focal point, and art created with macramé knots will build the focal point in any space. Having these intricate artworks will bring an aura to your space, and people will want to know where you got them from. The next time you buy pieces of art to decorate your house note that Macramé Knots are no longer your grandmother's art.

Cords are basically available in different thicknesses ranging from .5 to 8 mm. The larger the number, the thicker the cord, so 8 mm is the thickest. We can often use rings and beads crafted from silicone. A project is most easily worked on a flat macramé board. The project is carried out using t-pins, which aid in arranging the patterns of knots.

There is a broad range of colors, fabrics, and cord forms suitable for use in macramé, some synthetic and some natural. Indeed, almost everything where you could tie knots might be appropriate, and elements can be available in various places like hardware, craft, bricolage, sewing stores, and needlework. In some instances, the material chosen may be determined by what is going to be produced while, in some, it will be essential to play with your decisions because while there are cords widely utilized with some tasks that does not mean that some others do not perform quite as well.

CHAPTER 1:

What Is Macramé?

Macramé is a kind of fabric created using knotting (as opposed to weaving) methods. The first knots of macramé are the square (or coral reef knot) and forms of "hitching": numerous combinations of fifty percent hitches. It was long crafted by sailors, especially infancy or ornamental knotting kinds, to cover anything from knife deals with containers to parts of ships.

Reverse fifty percent hitches are sometimes made use of to preserve equilibrium when working left and also right fifty percent of a balanced item.

Natural leather or fabric belts are an additional device commonly created through macramé methods. A lot of friendship armbands traded among schoolchildren, and also teenagers are developed utilizing this approach. Suppliers at amusement parks, shopping malls, seasonal fairs, as well as various other public places may sell macramé jewelry or design as well.

The fundamental principle that includes jobs such as plant wall mounts and also owls. With a collection of blogs, I wish to present the knotting techniques, as well as start off with some simple tasks which I will create for you. We will certainly start with a description of the materials we will certainly utilize and also where they can be bought.

There are numerous sorts of cord utilized in macramé. Natural cables consist of jute and hemp. There is an all-natural charm to these cords, as well as they may be substituted in any of the tasks I show to you. My choice is to use just a synthetic rope, which is constructed from the herculean fiber. These cords are washable, as well as can likewise be cleaned and warm-fused. They are additionally discolored proof.

Cords are readily available in differing density varying from .5 to 8mm primarily; the larger the number, the thicker the cable, so 8mm is the thickest. We will, additionally, be using metal rings and beads. The most convenient way to work a job is on a level macramé board. The piece is held in the area, making use of t-pins, which assist with the spacing of knots in the patterns.

Hobby Lobby is a great area to grab vital supplies. They bring an excellent option for rings. They also have an appropriate selection of grains. They offer synthetic cord in 2 mm, 4 mm, as well as 6 mm, which are the densities I will certainly be using. Pepperell Braiding and also Kings Country are both sources online with the very best option. You can buy cord in numerous shades, including steel, Marbella, as well as bamboo rings, beads of all kinds, and macramé boards. It is best to save these places for bigger orders because of delivery costs.

Macramé is an approach to producing fabrics that use knots rather than weaving or knitting methods. Macramé was often utilized by seafarers to embellish products or their ships as well, as is additionally made use of to develop jewelry, bags, mats, plant hangers, and wall surface hangings. Occasionally, natural leather and also suede are used to produce macramé belts, as well as the relationship armbands made by several children, are created utilizing macramé.

There is a big series of knots as well as knot mixes utilized in macramé consisting of the square knot, fifty percent knot, fifty percent hitch, larks head knot, and also coil knot. Depending on the knots used, as well as whether they are used alone or combined with others, several layouts can be accomplished.

Do you know what you are wearing?

Armbands and other adornments can be produced using macramé, a sort of rope plaiting which keeps gemstones solidly set up. It is traced to the thirteenth century when Arabian weavers made knots known as "periphery" at lingered texture edges. Today, numerous specialties are deficient without macramé. What's more, here at Ivory Shoo, we utilize it for a large number of our armbands. Discover more benefits of macramé calfskin.

History of Macramé Leather

Arabia is the home of macramé. The calfskin and different materials were utilized toward the finish of texture. Next, it went into Spain and Turkey. What's more, in the fourteenth century, holy places in France and Italy utilized raised area materials made with macramé. Some accept that North American mariners made different kinds of knots with this calfskin.

Later on in the seventeenth and nineteenth centuries, the British received it and added to its general prevalence. A couple of years after this, America and China embraced it and utilized it to create style sacks, purses, flower holders, and different compartments.

Different knots can be made with the macramé calfskin: these incorporate half knot, square knot, two-fold half hitch, and overhand knot. Curiously, a lot more knots can be made from these essential and famous knots. In China, there are macramé knots known as "Good Luck" and "Monkey's Fist." Macramé materials incorporate cowhide, jute, shoelace, nylon, and rayon, among others.

Benefits of Macramé Leather

Because of the imagination that goes into the knotting of macramé, numerous individuals appreciate doing it for art. A few people accept that macramé is a symptomatic treatment for improving mental capacities, reinforcing arms and joints, improving focus, and quieting the brain. This, in any case, doesn't suggest that it requires no incredible creative skill. Utilizing macramé requires being feeling reflective and cautiously meshing the calfskin into knots and ropes. Macramé calfskin can likewise be used in many home and design items. Packs, attire, shoes, gems, entryway hangings, hanging bushels, and plant holders can be adorned with this great meshing.

At the point when utilized in wristbands, macramé looks stunning and characterizes your look. It further settles on an announcement about your choice of design extras, since it is a fundamental conviction that high-quality gems are regularly carefully made. For the most part, this excellent rope meshing is utilized to keep globules and gemstones together solidly and pleasantly. In like manner, it is flexible, adaptable, and versatile to numerous items. The flexibility of macramé makes it an ideal counterpart for bright gemstones and different dots that made armbands enchanting. Visit our assortments now for armbands made with macramé cowhide.

How an old Fiber Art has resurfaced as a Beautiful Craft

Knotting or macramé is one of the many specialties being resuscitated by the individuals who love working with their hands. Much the same as surface weaving, sewing, and embroidery are seeing a surge in popularity, macramé is being changed from a 1970s relic into a hot, in-vogue work of art.

An adaptable type of fiber artistry, macramé can be utilized to make everything from inside decorations and plant holders to adornments, totes, and in any event, dress things. Embellishments like glass or wooden dabs, like colored strings, can likewise open up a scope of imaginative prospects.

Become familiar with more about the intriguing history of macramé before jumping into essential procedures and guidance on the best way to begin making your own or buying some contemporary macramé.

Macramé's underlying foundations are very intriguing, with a history going back a great many years. Some accept that the term originates from the thirteenth-century Arabic word migramah, which signifies "periphery." Others take its sources to lie in the Turkish word macramé, which alludes to "napkin" or "towel," and was an approach to make sure about bits of weaving by utilizing many strings along the top or base of woven textures.

In any case, beautifying macramé, in reality, first shows up by the Babylonians and Assyrians that delineate bordered twisting used to enhance ensembles. In the thirteenth century, Arab weavers utilized enriching knots to complete the abundance string on shawls, cloaks, and towels.

While most consider macramé a fad of the 1970s, the art arrived at top notoriety in Victorian England. First acquainted with England in the late seventeenth century, Queen Mary herself taught classes to her women in-waiting. Most Victorian homes had some sort of macramé enhancement, as it was utilized not exclusively to adorn the dress yet, in addition, as drapes, tablecloths, and quilts. Given the skills at making knots, it should not shock anyone that mariners are, to a great extent, responsible for spreading macramé around the globe. It was an extraordinary method to take a break and could then be dealt with or sold when they docked, accordingly carrying it to territories like China and the New World. Loungers, belts, and ringer borders were a portion of the well-known things made by British and American mariners in the nineteenth century.

In the wake of losing fame, macramé saw a resurgence during the 1970s. It symbolized the Bohemian style and was utilized to make inside decorations, plant holders, adornments, and dress. The art, in the long run, disappeared in popularity, yet drifts will, in general, be much patterned. Presently, macramé is back, making waves again as inventive crafters think of contemporary patterns that have revived the notable knotting procedures.

CHAPTER 2:

Tools and Materials

Macramé Materials

Macramé stylists make use of different types of materials. The materials can be classified in two major ways: the natural materials and the synthetic materials.

Natural Materials

The qualities of natural materials differ from the synthetic material and knowing these qualities would help you to make better use of them. Natural cord materials existing today include Jute, Hemp, Leather, Cotton, Silk and Flax. There are also yarns made from natural fibers. Natural material fibers are made from plants and animals.

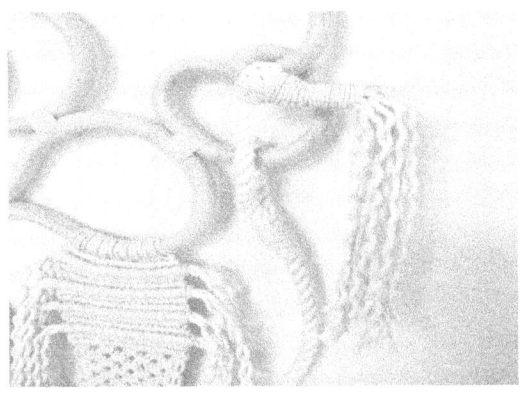

Synthetic Materials

Like natural materials, synthetic materials are also used in macramé projects. The fibers of synthetic materials are made through chemical processes. The major ones are nylon beading cord, olefin, satin cord and parachute cord.

Cord Measurement

Before you can embark on a macramé project, it is essential that you determine the amount of chord you will need. This includes knowing the length of the required cord and the total number of materials you have to purchase.

Equipment: to measure, you will need a paper for writing, pencil, tape rule and calculator. You would also need some basic knowledge of unit conversion as shared below:

1 inch = 25.4millimeters = 2.54 centimeters

1 foot =12 inches

1 yard = 3 feet = 36 inches

1 yard = 0.9 meters

Note: The circumference of a ring = 3.14 * diameter measured across the ring

Measuring Width

The first thing to do is determine the finished width of the widest area of your project. Once you have this width, pencil it down.

Next, determine the actual size of the materials, by measuring its width from edge to edge.

You can then proceed to determine the type of knot pattern you wish to use with the knowledge of the knot pattern. You must know the width and spacing (if required) of each knot. You should also determine if you want to add more cords to widen an area of if you would be needing extra cords for damps.

With the formula given above, calculate and determine the circumference of the ring of your designs.

Determine the mounting technique to be used. The cord can be mounted to a dowel, ring or other cord. Folded cords affect both the length and width of the cord measurement.

Cord Preparation

Though usually rarely emphasized, preparation of the cords and getting them ready for use in Macramé projects is one of the core pillars of the art of Macramé. At times, specialized processes such as conditioning and stiffening of cords need to be carried out before Macramé projects can be begun. In general, however, cord preparation in Macramé is mainly concerned with dealing with cut ends and preventing these ends from unraveling during the course of the project. During the course of a project, constant handing of materials can cause distortion in the ends which can end up having disastrous consequences on your project. Before starting your project, if you do not appropriately prepare particular kinds of cords, like ones that were made by the twisting of individual strands, that cord is likely to come apart, effectively wrecking your project.

Therefore, cord preparation is extremely and incomparably important to the success of any Macramé project, the preparation of each cord is meant to be done during the first step of making any knot, which is the step where you cut out your desired length of cord from the larger piece.

For cord conditioning, experts recommend rubbing beeswax along the length of the cord. To condition your cord, simply get a bit of beeswax, let it warm up a bit in your hands, and rub it along the cord's length. This will help prevent unwanted tight curls on your cord. Note that beeswax may be applied to both natural and synthetic materials. For synthetic materials however, only Satin and fine Nylon beading cords actually compulsorily require conditioning. After conditioning, inspect your cords for any imperfections and discard useless pieces to ensure the perfection of your project. After conditioning, then comes the actual process of cord preparation. Cords can be prepared (i.e. the ends can be prevented from fraying) through the use of a flame, a knot, tape and glue.

To prevent unraveling of your cord using a flame, firstly test a small piece of the material with the fire from a small lighter. The material needs to melt, not burn. If it burns, then such a cord is not suitable for flame preparation. To prepare using a flame, simply hold the cord to the tip of the fire for 2 to 5 seconds, make sure the cord does not ignite, but melts. Flame preparation is suitable for cords made from olefin, polyester and nylon, and the process is compulsory for the preparation of parachute cords.

Tying knots at the end of the cord is another effective method to prevent fraying. The Stevedore knot can be used in order to avoid fraying when using slippery materials. Glue is another priceless alternative that can be used to prevent fraying at the ends of cords efficiently. However, not all kinds of glue may be used in cord preparation. Only certain brands, such as the Alien's Stop Fray may be used in cord preparation. Household glue might also be used, but only when diluted with water. TO prepare your cord, simply rub the glue on the ends of the material and leave it to dry. If you intend to pass beads over the glued end, roll the cord's end between your fingers to make it narrower as it dries. Nail polish may also be used as an alternative to glue.

Tape is also a reliable method to prepare your cords. Make sure the end of the cord remains narrow by squeezing it between your fingers. It is advisable to use masking tape or cellophane tape for your preparations.

A particular class of Macramé cords, known as a parachute cord, requires a specific form of preparation. Parachute cords are composed of multiple core yarns surrounded by a braided sleeve. To prepare a parachute cord (also called a Paracord), pull out the core yarns from the sleeve, and expose the yarns by about half an inch. Now cut the core yarns back, so that they become even with the outer sleeve, and then push the sleeve forward till the yarns become invisible. To complete the preparation, apply flame to the outer sleeve till it melts, and then press the handle of your lighter onto the sleeve while it's still warm to flatten the area and keep it closed up. The melted area will look darker and more plastic than the rest of the material.

Finishing Techniques

Finishing techniques refer to the methods by which the ends of cords, after knots have been created may be taken care of to give a neat and tidy project. Finishing is often referred to as tying off. Several finishing knots are available and are incredibly effective methods for executing finishing processes. Reliable finishing knots include the overhand knot and the barrel knot.

Folding techniques are also dependable finishing techniques. For flexible materials like cotton, all you need to do is fold the ends flat against the back surface and add glue to the ends to hold them in place. For less flexible materials, fold the cords to the back, then pass them under a loop from one or more knots, and then apply glue, allow it to dry, and cut off excess material.

Finally, you can do your finishing with the aid of fringes. You may choose between a brushed fringe and a beaded fringe.

Adding Cords

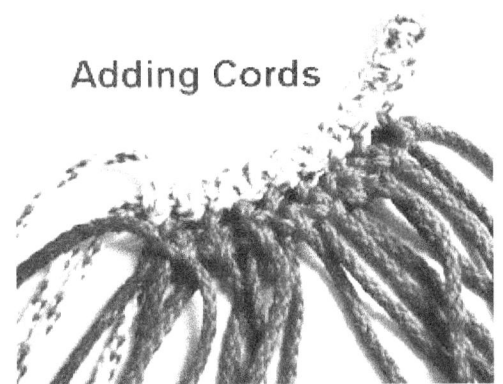

During Macramé projects, you would continuously be faced by the need to add a cord to an existing cord or any other surface such as a ring or a dowel. The process of adding cords to surfaces is usually called mounting. To add extra cords to a ring or dowel, the most common technique to use is the Reverse Larks Head Knot. When adding cords to already existing cords in use, however, it is essential that the new cords blend into the overall design. To prevent lopsidedness of the pattern, it is also crucial to add an equal number of cords to both sides in some projects. It is also essential to avoid gaps when adding new cords. You can add new cords to an already existing cord using the square knot, the linked overhand knot and of course the regular overhand knot. Other techniques used for adding cords include the diamond stitch and the triangle knot.

CHAPTER 3:

Types of Macramé (Knots, Tricks, Cords)

Types of Macramé Knots

Capuchin Knot

This knot for any project, and can be used as the foundation for the base of the project. Use lightweight cord for this – it can be purchased at craft stores or online, wherever you get your macramé supplies.

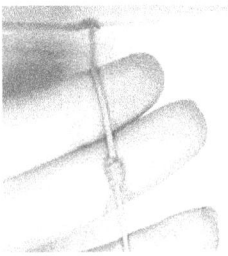

Don't rush, and make sure you have even tension throughout. Practice makes perfect, but with the illustrations to help you, you'll find it's not hard at all to create.

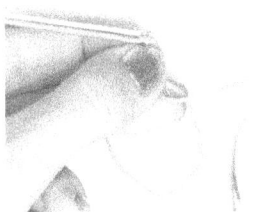

Start with the base cord, tying the knot onto this and working your way along the project.

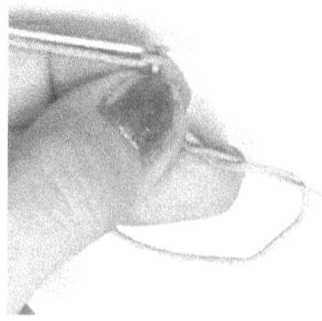

Twist the cord around itself 2 times, pulling the string through the center to form the knot.

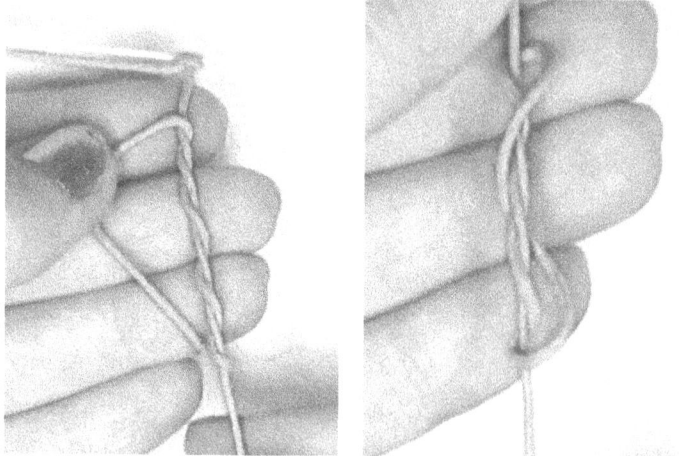

It is going to take practice before you are able to get it perfectly each time, but remember that practice does make perfect, and with time, you are going to get it without too much trouble.

Make sure all is even and secure, and tie off. Snip off all the loose ends, and you are ready to go!

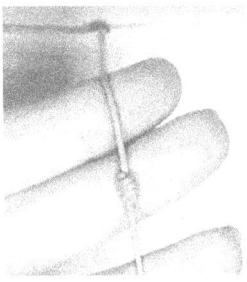

Crown Knot

This is an excellent beginning knot for any project, and can be used as the foundation for the base of the project. Use lightweight cord for this – it can be purchased at craft stores or online, wherever you get your macramé supplies.

Don't rush, and make sure you have even tension throughout. Practice makes perfect, but with the illustrations to help you, you'll find it's not hard at all to create.

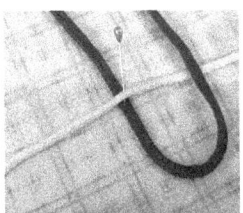

Use a pin to help keep everything in place as you are working.

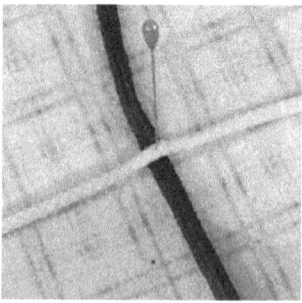

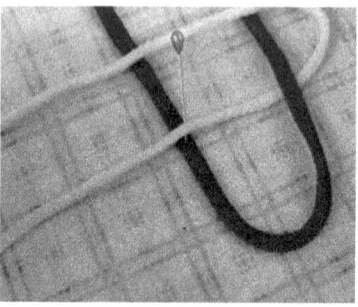

Weave the strings in and out of each other as you can see in the photos. It helps to practice with different colors to help you know what is going on.

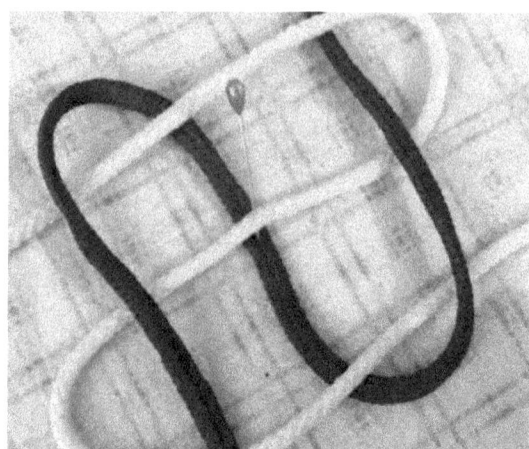

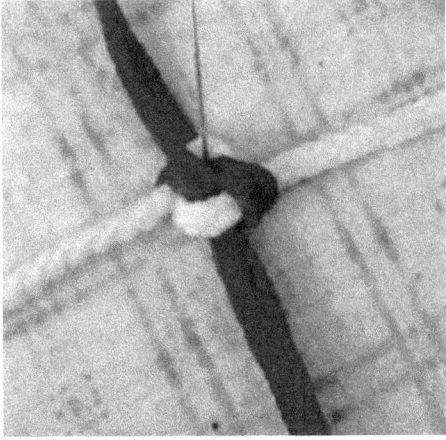

Pull the knot tight, then repeat for the next row on the outside.

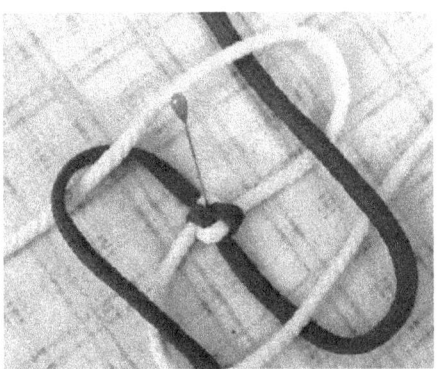

Continue to do this as often as you like to create the knot. You can make it as thick as you want, depending on the project. You can also create more than one length on the same cord.

It is going to take practice before you are able to get it perfectly each time, but remember that practice does make perfect, and with time, you are going to get it without too much trouble.

Make sure all is even and secure, and tie off. Snip off all the loose ends, and you are ready to go!

Diagonal Double Half Knot

This is the perfect knot to use for basket hangings, decorations, or any projects that are going to require you to put weight on the project. Use a heavier weight cord for this, which you can find at craft stores or online.

Don't rush, and make sure you have even tension throughout. Practice makes perfect, but with the illustrations to help you, you'll find it's not hard at all to create.

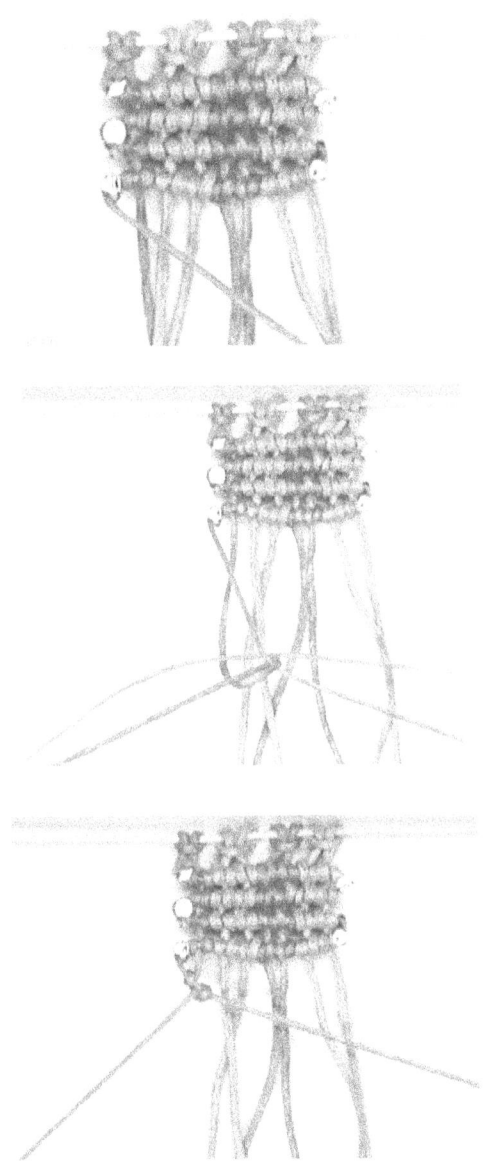

Keep it even as you work your way throughout the piece. Tie the knots at 4 inch intervals, working your way down the entire thing.

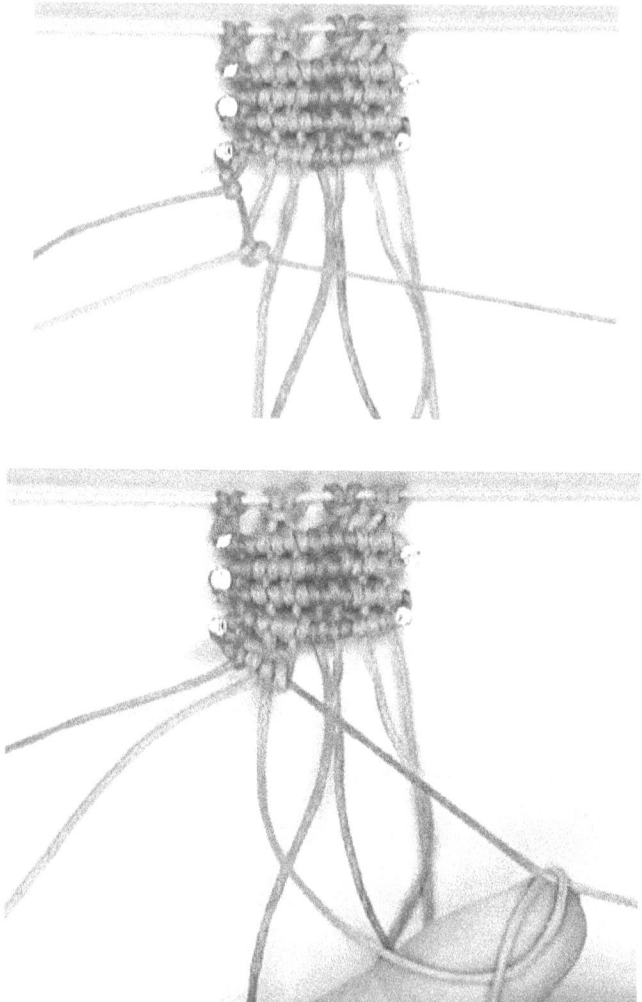

Weave in and out throughout, watching the photo as you can see for the right placement of the knots.

Again, it helps to practice with different colors so you can see what you need to do throughout the piece.

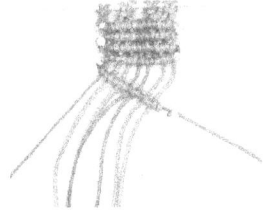

It is going to take practice before you are able to get it perfectly each time, but remember that practice does make perfect, and with time, you are going to get it without too much trouble.

Make sure all is even and secure, and tie off. Snip off all the loose ends, and you are ready to go!

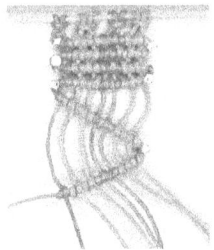

Frivolite Knot

This is an excellent beginning knot for any project, and can be used as the foundation for the base of the project. Use lightweight cord for this – it can be purchased at craft stores or online, wherever you get your macramé supplies.

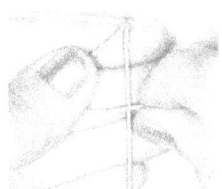

Don't rush, and make sure you have even tension throughout. Practice makes perfect, but with the illustrations to help you, you'll find it's not hard at all to create.

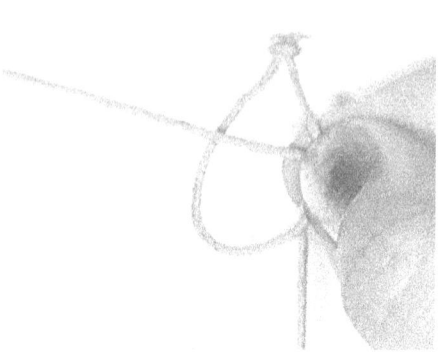

Use the base string as the guide to hold it in place, then tie the knot onto this. This is a very straightforward knot, watch the photo and follow the directions you see.

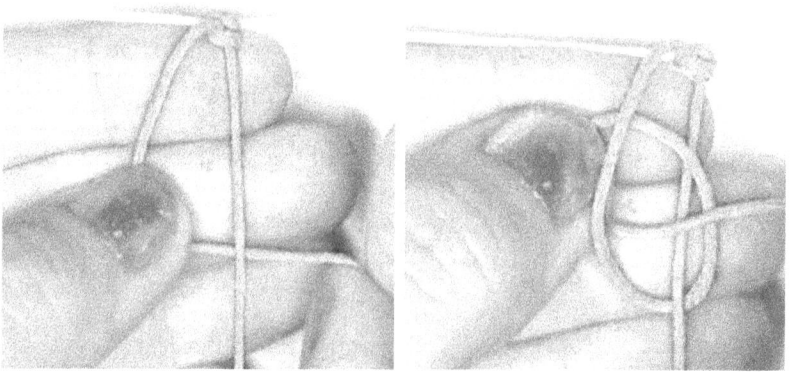

Pull the end of the cord up and through the center.

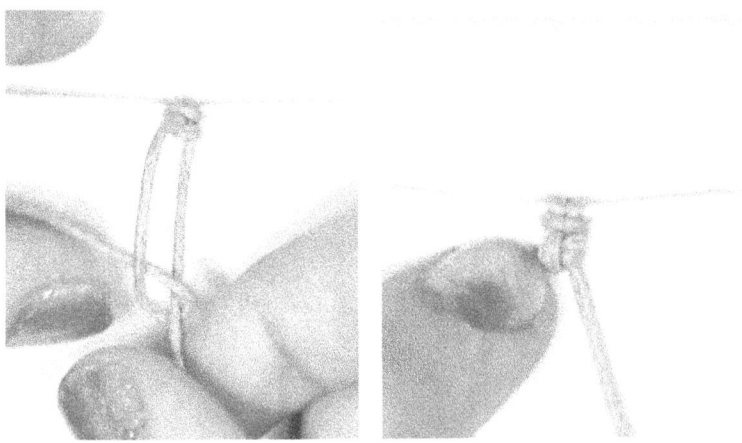

It is going to take practice before you are able to get it perfectly each time, but remember that practice does make perfect, and with time, you are going to get it without too much trouble.

Make sure all is even and secure, and tie off. Snip off all the loose ends, and you are ready to go!

Horizontal Double Half Knot

This is an excellent beginning knot for any project, and can be used as the foundation for the base of the project. Use lightweight cord for this – it can be purchased at craft stores or online, wherever you get your macramé supplies.

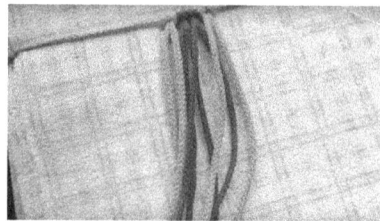

Don't rush, and make sure you have even tension throughout. Practice makes perfect, but with the illustrations to help you, you'll find it's not hard at all to create.

Keep it even as you work your way throughout the piece. Tie the knots at 4 inch intervals, working your way down the entire thing.

It is going to take practice before you are able to get it perfectly each time, but remember that practice does make perfect, and with time, you are going to get it without too much trouble.

Make sure all is even and secure, and tie off. Snip off all the loose ends, and you are ready to go!

Josephine Knot

This is the perfect knot to use for basket hangings, decorations, or any projects that are going to require you to put weight on the project. Use a heavier weight cord for this, which you can find at craft stores or online.

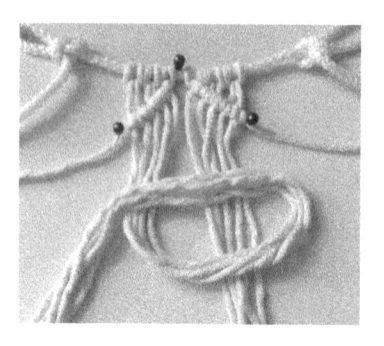

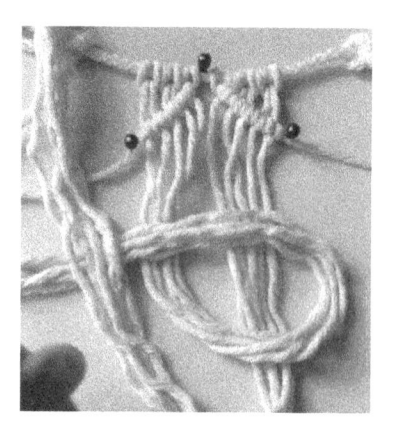

Don't rush, and make sure you have even tension throughout. Practice makes perfect, but with the illustrations to help you, you'll find it's not hard at all to create.

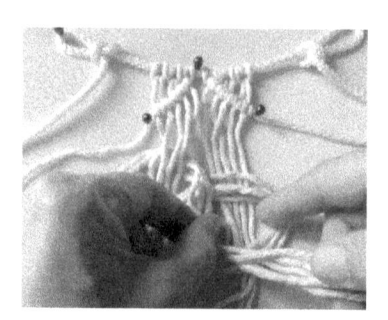

Use the pins along with the knots that you are tying, and work with more extensive areas all at the same time. This is going to help you keep the project in place as you continue to work throughout the piece.

Pull the ends of the knots through the loops, and form the ring in the center of the strings.

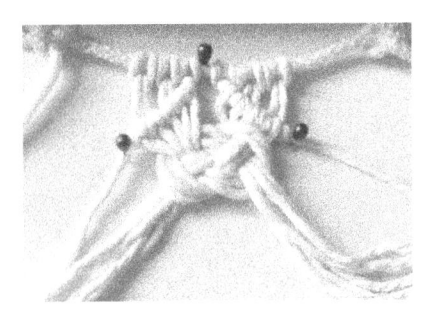

It is going to take practice before you are able to get it perfectly each time, but remember that practice does make perfect, and with time, you are going to get it without too much trouble.

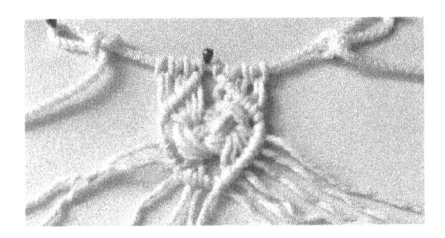

Make sure all is even and secure, and tie off. Snip off all the loose ends, and you are ready to go!

Lark's Head Knot

This is an excellent beginning knot for any project, and can be used as the foundation for the base of the project. Use lightweight cord for this

– it can be purchased at craft stores or online, wherever you get your macramé supplies.

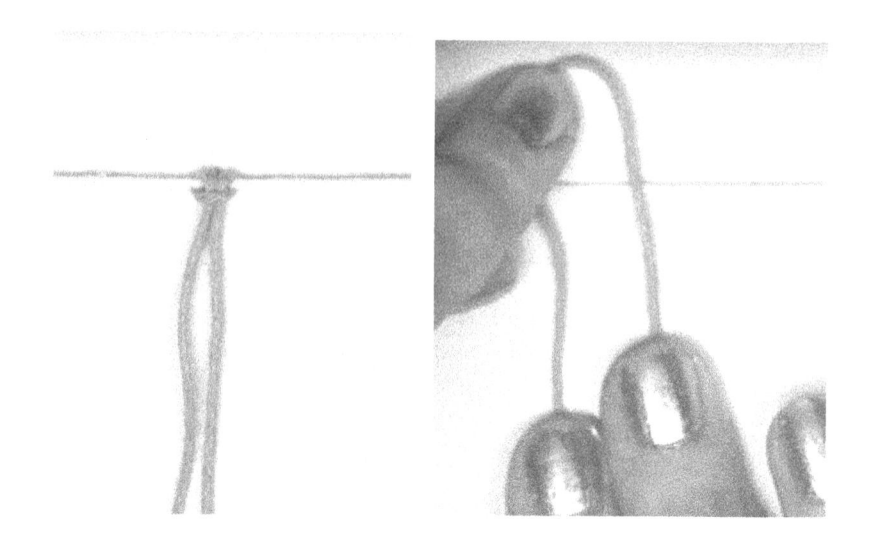

Don't rush, and make sure you have even tension throughout. Practice makes perfect, but with the illustrations to help you, you'll find it's not hard at all to create.

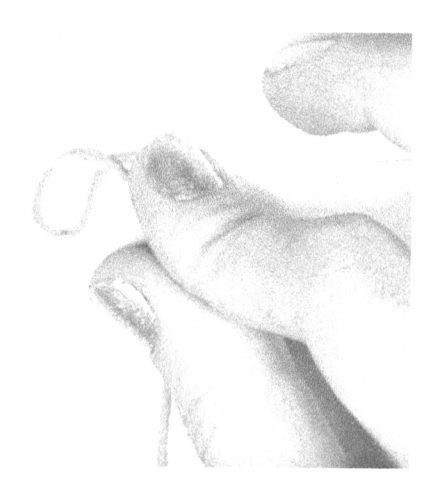

Use the base string as the core part of the knot, working around the end of the string with the cord. Make sure all is even as you loop the string around the base of the cord.

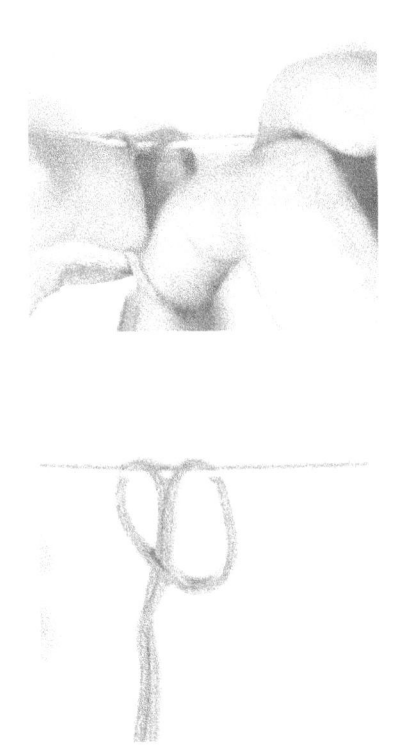

Create a slip knot around the base of the string and keep both ends even as you pull the cord through the center of the piece.

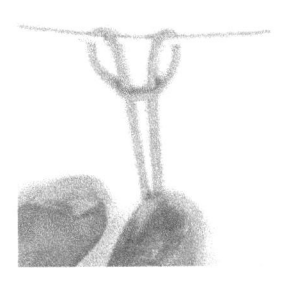

It is going to take practice before you are able to get it perfectly each time, but remember that practice does make perfect, and with time, you are going to get it without too much trouble.

Make sure all is even and secure, and tie off. Snip off all the loose ends, and you are ready to go!

Reverse Lark's Head Knot

This is an excellent beginning knot for any project, and can be used as the foundation for the base of the project. Use lightweight cord for this – it can be purchased at craft stores or online, wherever you get your macramé supplies.

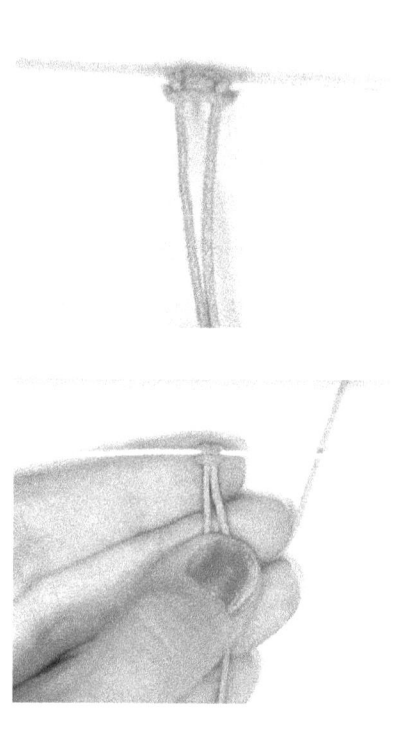

Don't rush, and make sure you have even tension throughout. Practice makes perfect, but with the illustrations to help you, you'll find it's not hard at all to create.

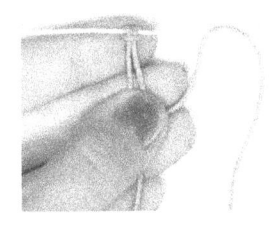

Use two hands to make sure that you have everything even and tight as you work. You can use tweezers if it helps to make it tight against the base of the string.

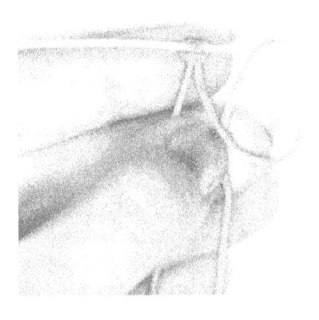

Use both hands to pull the string evenly down against the base string to create the knot.

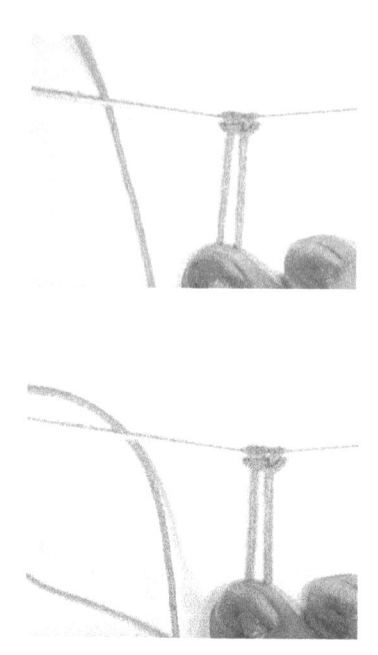

Again, keep the base even as you pull the center, creating the firm knot against your guide cord.

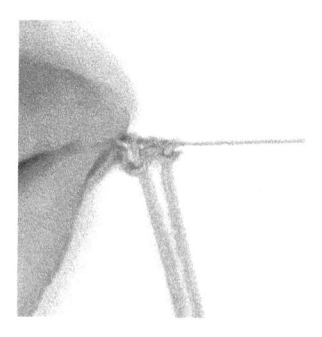

It is going to take practice before you are able to get it perfectly each time, but remember that practice does make perfect, and with time, you are going to get it without too much trouble.

CHAPTER 4:

Other Knots

The Hangman's Noose

To make the Knot

1. Use a piece of cord or rope that is at least 3 ft. long

2. Place the cord on a flat surface and form an "S" shape with the bottom or lead part of the cord left long, this is so you have something to tie it to when it's finished.

3. Poke the end of the cord through the top of the loop.

Adjust the noose until it's the size you want, and the coils look nice and tight.

To make a Single Rope Knot Ladder

This simple knot ladder can be used as an emergency fire escape or as an aid for use in a child's tree house.

To make the Ladder

1. Place a single length of cord on a flat surface and form it into a "U" shape.

2. Place the cord between your two hands and form it into an "S" shape. Then push the "S" down by bringing your hands together

3. To make the first row of your ladder, take the left end of the cord and thread it through the first, left bend of the "S." Bring the end of the cord under the bottom curve and wrap it around the whole "S" four times.

To Make a Rope Ladder with Wooden Rungs

1. First lay the cord flat on the ground and make an overhand loop around 15 inches (38 cm) from the top-end.

2. Pull the standing part of the cord through the overhead loop, by putting your fingers through the underside of the loop and grasping the standing part of the cord. This should form a new loop.

3. Insert your wooden rung into the new loop and set it at the desired position and tighten the rope. The knot should be visible above and below the rung

4. Tie an overhand knot by making an overhand loop, then passing the working end over, then through the loop. Ensure that the overhand knot is directly underneath the knot that is supporting the rung.

5. Repeat steps for the other piece of rope that will be used as the other side of the ladder. Taking care to make sure that your rungs are level and even.

6. The rung should be started by placing the overhand loop anywhere from 9 to 15 inches (23 to 38cm) from the wooden rung, it depends on the height of the people who may use the ladder, shorter distance for children and longer for adults The rungs should all be spaced uniformly, and distanced to suit those using it comfortably.

7. The ladder should be secured at the top using one of the knots described in a timber hitch.

8. Securing the ladder at the bottom is optional but ensuring it will significantly increase its stability and make it easier to climb.

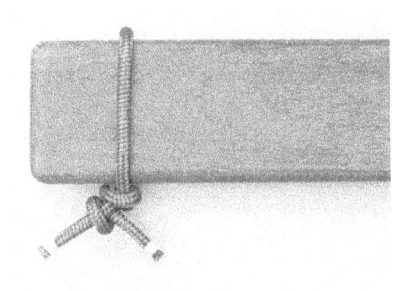

Butcher's Knot

Butcher's knot is used in numerous situations. When tied it creates the first loop around the sack or pack. It is also used in preparing roasts or meat. When you make the first loop it shouldn't go down around the object. Its advantage is, when tightened correctly, its working end looks like a ring which makes it not so easy to untie.

Butcher's knot is so easy to tie, and it can be done so fast that, observing professional butchers it is almost impossible to catching all the steps of it. It requires using very little string because knot can be created while its end is still attached to the coil. Butcher's knot is a knot when used for its purposes.

To make Butcher's knot:

1. At its standing end make an Overhand knot and pull firmly.
2. When you create the loop around your fingers, put the circle against the short end.
3. Take both ends and tie them firmly to create the knot.
4. Once done, cut the long end.

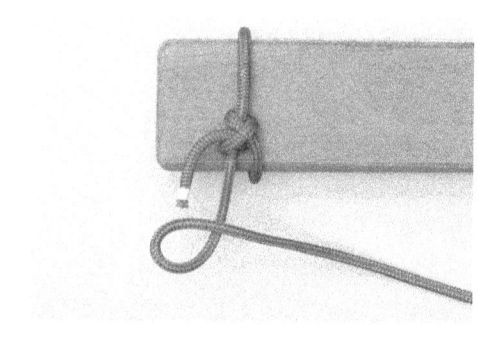

Corned Beef

Corned beef - as its name says - is usually used as a binding knot for beef meat while it is prepared. It is often made in a smaller string or line. Due to the fact that beef meat often shrinks during preparation, needs to be tied at intervals and it will still hold in between while the meat is cooking.

To make Corned beef knot

1. First, create the Buntline hitch and tie it firmly to the standing part.

2. Buntline needs to slide along the standing part so it will be tied in the process of preparation of meat.

3. After making sure that the beef is full shrunk go with the half hitch around the working end.

How to Hogtie Someone

To hogtie someone correctly is not something anyone would normally do for fun as being tied in that position is usually very uncomfortable and not a pleasant experience to have, unless of course you are into kinky stuff and using soft restraints, but that's another story.

The most practical rope or cord to use to tie someone up is solid-braid nylon rope in 7/16" or 3/8" in diameter, these types of cord are available from most hardware or building supply stores. They, unlike many other types of cord or ropes have minimal stretch and the knots will stay easy to untie even after you pull them around.

Being hogtied, a person is totally incapacitated, with almost no chance of escape or even putting up any real resistance. When hogtied, a person's hands and feet are tied behind their back as well as being tied together, often with additional ties around the chest and thighs, most often the person is also gagged and blindfolded. It can be very dangerous to leave anyone unattended when hogtied, especially people who are elderly, overweight or unfit.

To make the hogtie

- The first step when you hogtie someone is to tie their hands behind their back, this can be done in several ways:

1. Tie the hands with the palms together this is the most comfortable for the victim.

2. Tie the hands with the wrists crossed and with the palms out, this is often uncomfortable for the victim.

3. Tie the arms together at the elbows behind the back and also secure the wrists. Often this is the most uncomfortable position, especially if the victim is large and overweight.

4. Wrap the cord around the wrists several times, then wrap it several times between the fingers and wrist, pull it tight and make a hitch knot.

5. If you want to secure the arms first (this is advisable if the victim is struggling)

Tie the elbows by wrapping the cord several times around the arms just above the elbows and then several times between the lower arms and through the gape above the elbows, pull it tight and make a hitch knot. (Often, especially with large, overweight people it is not possible to bring their elbows together, behind their backs because of physical limitations. In this event tie the elbows in the manner described for tying a rope handcuff as is explained in following knot description) Then tie the wrists either palm together or facing outwards.

6. In case you want to make the hogtie a little more secure when you tie the wrists pass the rope several times around the torso as well, and holding the arms in place, so the victim is unable to lift them up or down, secure the ropes with an overhand knot.

- Tie the feet by first removing the shoes and socks, then wrap the cord around the ankles several times, then through the gap above the ankles, between the legs and between the feet.

1. If the person is struggling, a good option is to first tie their legs together just under the knee, by wrapping the cord around their legs several times, then passing it between their lower legs and around and through the gap between their upper legs. If you apply pressure to the toes and fingers, especially against the normal movement of the joints, you can very quickly bring any captive to submission and

control. The degree of pressure is determined by their amount of refusal to cooperate.

- The final step of applying the hogtie is to tie the wrists and ankles together behind the back. This is best done with a separate cord. First pass the cord through the ankle ties and then the wrist ties, pulling them together and bringing the ankles up by bending the person's knees. The ideal way to leave a person tied using this method is to have the soles of their feet facing you if you stand in front of them looking down their body. They can be left in this position or moved onto their side. In order to prevent the hogtie causing damage to the person and restricting the blood flow they should be continuously monitored.

To Make A Rope Handcuff

Rope handcuffs are quick and easy to make, there are several differences between handcuffing a willing partner for games and securing an unwilling person to restrict their movements. This description is for a willing partner, but the same principle applies to a reluctant or struggling person. If the handcuffs are for fun using soft linen or silk type rope or wrap is ideal, otherwise use solid-braid nylon rope of 7/16" or 3/8" in diameter

To make the Handcuff

About 25tf (8.5M) of cord is needed to make these handcuffs

- First have the person hold their hands about about 2 fist spaces apart

- Drape the cord over their wrists so there is an even overhang on each side

- This will result in the victim's wrists being loosely wrapped.

- Bring the right and left cords under the wrists into the middle and cross them over each other in the center

- Then, starting with the right cord, wrap it tightly around the center between the wrists and continue winding or wrapping, moving the coils from the center to the outside or towards the wrists.

- Repeat with the left thread, winding or wrapping in the opposite direction from the center to the wrists.

- You should make an even number of coils or wraps on each side and finish when there is a small gap between the cord and the skin. Check to see if the knot is too tight or maybe too loose; adjust it by twisting each side in the direction you wound it to tighten or the other way to loosen.

- If you desire, you can make several more turns or tie it off there.

- Lift the last loop on the right side and tuck the end of the cord through the resulting circle from inside to out. Repeat on the other side to finish tying it off, then pull on both ends of rope to make it secure.

- Any remaining cord can be cut off tucked in or used to tie the victim up to an activity area.

CHAPTER 5:

Things to Look For In Choosing a Macramé Cord

We should start by characterizing what the macramé cord is.

Macramé string is a group of fibers/strands turned or braided together, and is then used to be knotted or tied to shape a material art known as macramé.

Huge numbers of you who are merely starting will frequently peruse or hear macramé lines as either macramé cord, yarn, or threads. Intermittently, the macramé cord is utilized conversely with these synonyms.

Picking Macramé Cord

That way, you can pick the right string for your future macramé projects.

At the point when I previously began macramé, I had no clue there was various kinds of lines. I accepted the macramé line was plain Jane cord, and it was what was expected to make macramé. I didn't know there was a wide range of strands that could be utilized for your projects. Much to my dismay at that point, not all macramé line is made equal.

Let us separate it. The three distinct kinds of Macramé string are:

- Interlaced
- 3-utilize/3 Strand
- Single Strand

Most of the macramé projects you see online will frequently be categorized as one of these classes.

Macramé Braided Cord

Braided or likewise referred to as Macramé cord is your run of the mill macramé cord that you'll discover at your big box retail locations, Hobby Lobby, Michaels, and even Wall-mart.

Most macramé beginners will begin by buying braided cord since it is the most reasonable and least demanding way to start macramé. By and large, it is braided string accessible at most art stores and huge box retailers. The vast majority rush to their neighborhood store to purchase whatever line they can discover when they need to begin immediately. In the wake of finishing a couple of macramé projects, they will rapidly find a braided line isn't the most reasonable kind of line for making macramé. This is because the twisted cord is a cord made up independently or a blend of cotton, nylon, polyester, polypropylene, or other solid fibers. It's extraordinary to integrate things and give them a solid hold, yet it is hard to un-knot and fringe with.

Utilizing a braided cord is not a terrible place to begin. It takes care of business, and you can wind up with an appropriately completed project.

As a general rule, you'll end up changing to either 3-utilize or the most customarily utilized macramé string – single strandline.

You may frequently hear the utilization of macramé rope and cord. They are ordinarily talking about an equal thing. How I separate between the two is that cord is commonly braided, or 3-utilize string and cord is a widely inclusive term for fibers, string, and cord.

Macramé 3-Ply/3-Stands Cord

3-ply is likewise referred to as 3-stands cord. It is comprised of 3 smaller strands into a long turned cord. You will frequently hear macramé artists talk about utilizing 3-employ or 4-handle macramé string, and those just methods the number of strands contorted together to frame one single strand of string. Underneath, you'll have the option to observe the distinction between 3-Ply and 4-Ply outwardly.

Bochiknot Macramé Cotton Cord 3ply, 4ply, 3mm, 4mm, 5mm, 6mm, 7mm

When you begin getting into macramé lines that are multiple strands, this is what is referred to as multi-utilize, where you can have 4, 5, or 6-strands all spun together to shape one strand. There are 4 strands curved along to frame a single strand of cord.

Macramé Single Strand Cord

Single strand cotton line is by a wide margin the best sort of macramé string to browse if you are choosing to get into macramé as a customary hobby or full-time gig. Single strand string usually is more costly, and in this way, if you would prefer not to spend too much immediately on the costly string, locate some less expensive cotton cord on amazon and start with those. As long as it is agreeable on the hands, it will be extraordinary to gain from. It will make it a lot simpler cutting line, knotting hitches, unraveling knots, and bordering the line.

Macramé Cord Composition

The makeup of the macramé string falls into 2 sections, natural or synthetic fibers.

Characteristic fibers are strands delivered usually in the earth. They are provided by plants, animals, or geographical procedures. Instances of individual fibers are cotton, wool, cloth, jute, and hemp.

These strands can be usually separated and reused.

The other option is synthetic fibers. Manufactured strands are produced using synthesized polymers of little atoms. The mixes used to make these fibers originate from raw materials, such as oil-based synthetic compounds or petrochemicals. Instances of manufactured fibers are nylon, polyester, and spandex.

Macramé Cord Texture

Macramé feel, touch, appearance, finish, and surface

If you have seen a variety of macramé cords, you will know each spool of the line has another vibe, finish, and surface to it. Getting a feeling of the various sorts of cord surfaces is a significant part of realizing your macramé cords.

The more macramé pieces you make, the rapidly you'll find surfaces assume a tremendous job in the entirety of your macramé projects.

If you're going to make a buy on a macramé line on the internet, attempt various brand providers and see what surface fits you. You will find that not all macramé cotton threads are made equivalent. The exterior and feel to the threads may change from one provider to the next.

Macramé Cord Size

Realizing string size is likewise significant while doing your ideal macramé project. The size of the line assumes a vital job in the visual appearance of macramé projects.

If you're interested, we have another article that goes over the macramé cord's different sizes. What size of the Macramé cord do I use for my projects?

For simplicity, the macramé cord can be separated into 3 size classes – little, medium, and big.

Little Macramé Cord – is commonly your 1-2 mm width size string. You'll regularly discover these threads utilized in making jewelry to string through beads, catches, and little definite craft projects.

Medium Macramé Cord – is the place you will discover most of all macramé projects are made. These sizes are periodically utilized for plant hangers, inside decorations, lights, curtains, floor coverings, and so forth.

Big Macramé Cord – This will be your BIG macramé pieces. This will be in the scope of anything 6mm or more. For the most part, these big sizes are utilized to cover vast regions of the room. You will see the knots tend as less, however, a lot bigger.

What Cord Do You Use For Macramé?

The most straightforward answer is: it depends.

I would suggest utilizing 3mm-4mm Single Strand Cotton Cord. If you have attempted a couple of projects using less expensive line and you're currently open to putting resources into some more pleasant line for better quality activities, at that point, single strand string might be directly for you.

The motivation behind why I would suggest utilizing a single strandline is because it will improve your macramé experience. Knotting hitches and disentangling them will be, to a lesser degree, a battle. Cutting lines and bordering won't need to feel like hard work, and above all, your macramé tasks will come out stylishly satisfying.

CHAPTER 6:

Macramé Plant Hangers

Macramé Plant Hanger

Description: Plant hanger of 2 feet and 5.5 inches (75 cm)

Knots: Square knot, alternating square knot, half knot and gathering knot.

Supplies:

- Cord: 10 strands of cord of 18 feet and 0.5 inches (5, 5 meter), 2 strands of 3 feet and 3.3 inches (1 meter)
- Ring: 1 round ring (wood) of 1.6 inches (4 cm) diameter
- Container: 7 inches (18 cm) diameter

Directions (step-by-step):

1. Fold the 10 long strands of cord in half through the wooden ring.

2. Tie all (now 20) strands together with 1 shorter strand with a gathering knot. Hide the cut cord ends after tying the gathering knot.

3. Make a square knot using all cords: use from each side 4 strands to make the square knot; the other 12 strands stay in the middle.

4. Divide the strands in 2 sets of 10 strands each. Tie a square knot in each set using 3 strands on each side (4 strands stay in the middle of each group).

5. Divide the strands in 3 sets of 6 strands for the outer groups and 8 strands for the group in the middle. Tie a square knot in each set using 2 strands on each side.

6. Divide the strands into 5 sets of 4 strands each and make a square knot with each set.

7. Continue with the 5 sets. In the 2 outer sets you tie 4 square knots and in the 3 inner sets, you tie 9 half knots.

8. Using all sets tie 7 alternating square knots by connecting two strands in each set with the right two strands of the set next to it. In the first, third, fifth and seventh row you are not using the 2 outer strands on each side.

9. Repeat step 7 and 8. In repeating step 8 you tie 5 alternating square knots instead of 7 alternating square knots.

10. To help you with the next steps, number the strands from left to right, numbering them no.1 to no. 20.

11. With the 4 middle strands (no. 9 tot 12) you make 14 square knots.

12. Make a square knot with the set of 4 strands no. 3 to 6 and the set of 4 strands no. 15 to 18.

13. Divide the strands into 4 sets of 4 strands (ignore the set with the 14 square knots in the middle) and tie 12 square knots in each set.

14. Drop down 2 inches (5 cm).

15. Make 5 sets in the following way and tie in each set a square knot:

a. Set 1 consists out of strands no. 5, 6, 1 and 2

b. Set 2 consists out of strands no. 3, 4, 9 and 10

c. Set 3 consists out of strands no. 7, 7, 13 and 14

d. Set 4 consists out of strands no. 11, 12, 17 and 18

e. Set 5 consists out of strands no. 19, 20, 16 and 15

16. Drop down another 2 inches (5 cm), no knots. If you need to leave more space without knots in order to fit your container, you can do so

17. Gather all strands together and then tie a gathering knot with the left-over shorter strand. Trim all strands at different lengths to finish your project.

Macramé Plant Hanger II

Cord: 8 strands of cords of each 26 feet and 3 inches (8 meter), 1 short strand of cord

Description: Plant hanger of 4 feet and 3 inches (1, 30 meter)

Knots: Square knot, alternating square knot, half knot, alternating half hitch, gathering knot.

Supplies:

- Wooden Ring: 1 round ring (wood) of 1, 6 inches (4 cm) diameter
- Container/Flowerpot: 7 inches (18 cm) diameter

Directions (step-by-step):

1. Fold 8 strands of cord, the long ones, in half over and through the ring. Now you have 16 strands of cord in total. Group them in sets of four strands.

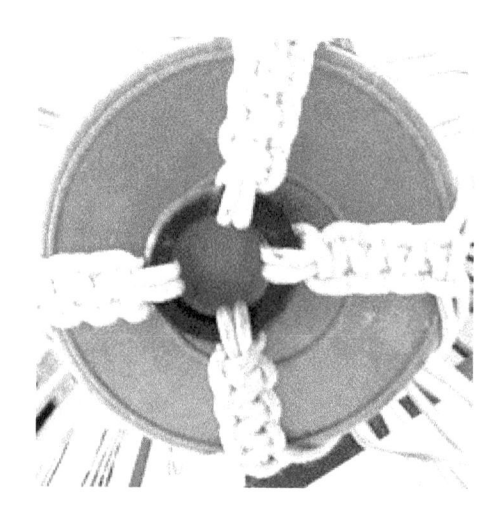

2. Tie 4 square knots on each set of four strands.

3. Drop down 3.15 inches (8 cm)

4. Tie a row of 4 square knots to connect the left two strands in each set with the right two of the set next to it. Repeat on each of the 4 sets.

5. Drop down 4.3 inches (11 cm).

6. Repeat step 4, starting with the 2 right strands this time.

7. Take 2 strands of 1 set and make 10 alternating half hitch knots. Repeat for the 2 left strands of that set. Repeat for all sets.

8. Drop down 3.9 inches (10 cm) and tie a row of 48 half knots on each set of four strands.

9. Take the 2 middle strands of each set and make 8 alternating half hitch knots. You leave the 2 strands on the side of the set as they are (without knots).

10. Tie a row of 30 half knots on each set of four strands.

11. Use a new short strand of cord to make a gathering knot around all strands.

12. Cut off and fray the ends as desired.

Macramé Plant Hanger III

Description: Plant hanger of 2 feet and 5.5 inches (75 cm)

Knots: Square knot, alternating square knot, crown knot, gathering knot and overhand knot.

Supplies:

- Cord: 4 strands of cord of 13 feet and 1.5 inches (4 meter), 4 strands of 16 feet and 4.8 inches (5 meter), 2 strands of 3 feet and 3.4 inches (1 meter)
- Ring: 1 round ring (wood) of 1.5 inches (4 cm) diameter
- Beads: wooden beads
- Cristal Bowl/Container: 7 inches (18 cm) diameter

Directions (step-by-step):

1. Fold the 8 long strands of cord (4 strands of 13 feet and 1.5 inches and 4 strands of 16 feet and 4.8 inches) in half through the wooden ring

2. Tie all (now 16) strands together with 1 shorter strand with a gathering knot. Hide the cut cord ends after tying the gathering knot.

3. Divide the strands into 4 sets of 4 strands each. Each set has 2 long strands and 2 shorter strands.

Tie 5 Chinese crown knots in each set. Pull each strand tight and smooth.

4. Tie 8 square knots on each set of four strands. In each set the 2 shorter strands are in the middle and you are tying with the 2 outer, longer strands.

5. Tie 15 half square knots with each set.

6. Drop down 5.5 inches (14 cm), no knots, and tie an alternating square knot.

7. Drop down 3.15 inches (8 cm) and tie again an alternating square knot with 4 strands.

8. Drop down 1.5 inches (4 cm). Put into container/bowl into the hanger to make sure it will fit, gather all strands together and then tie a gathering knot with the left-over shorter strand. Add a bead to each strand end (optional). Tie an overhand knot in each stran and trim all strands just below the overhand knots.

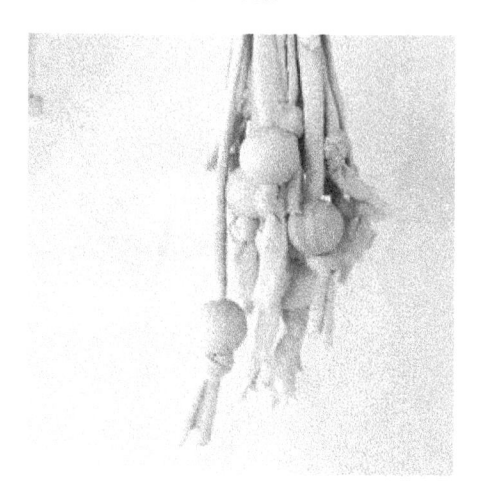

CHAPTER 7:

Wall Hangings

Materials Needed for Macramé Wall Hanging

- Macramé Rope– I have been using this 4 mm rope– 12– 16' (as in feet) cords are required (twelve). Note that this is a thick hanging wall, which is why we need longer cords. To act as your hanger, you will also need 1 shorter piece of cording. Simply tie it on either end with a simple knot.

- A dowel or a stick– I used a long (ha-ha) knitting needle. As long as it is straight and robust and as long as you need to work with what you have!

- Basic macramé knots were used for this wall hanging pattern:

1. Square Knot and Alternating Knot
2. Half Hitch Knot

Here Is the Step-By-Step Guide for Macramé Hanging Wall.

Begin by folding in half your 16' cords. Make sure that the ends are the same. Place the cord loop under the dowel and thread through the loop the ends of the rope. Pull closely. That's the Head Knot of your first Reverse Lark. (For assistance, refer to basic macramé knots). Repeat with the other 11 cords.

First make 2 Square Knots rows. Now make 2 rows of Square Knots Alternating. Now make 2 more Square knots sets. Follow this pattern until you have 10 rows in total (2 rows of knots in square, 2 rows of square knots in alternation). Working from left to right– make two half-hitch knots across your piece in a diagonal pattern. Now, from right to left– make double half-hitch knots across your piece in a diagonal pattern. You should have been working your way back to the left.

Make 2 more rows of knots of square. We will finish the hanging wall with a set of spiral knots– This is basically a half-square node sequence (or left-side square branch). (Do not end on the right side of the knot, just make square knots and spiral on the left side for you again and again.)

To build this spiral, I made a total of 13 half square knots. Finally– I trimmed in a straight line the bottom cords. The total size for the hanging of my wall is 6.5" wide by 34.

DIY Round Macramé Boho Coasters

I don't seem to be able to rest every time I find a craft idea, until I know how to do that, these coasters are the perfect example, I've done a macramé bracelet before, but to make a macramé round is strange for me. After exploring the internet, finding some confusing posts and making my first coaster after ways to create it. That's the way I found it easier (although there's another one I tested as well) and it also got me the most beautiful result.

Supplies:

- 3 mm cotton cord
- Something to hold the cords, a cork coaster or a board, either tape or as I used it.
- Pins to hold if the cork is used.
- Fabric Scissors
- Ruler or measuring tape
- Comb

Boho Christmas Trees

Cut the yarn in 7-8-inch bits. Take two strands and fold them in half in order to form a loop. Place one of the loops under a twig. Start with the bowed end of the other strand and move the ends of the strand under the twig through the loop.

DIY Bohemian Macramé Mirror Wall Hanging

In the art of macramé, there are so many knots and ways to tie them, it can seem daunting and easy to avoid. I had an eye on a macramé mirror type plant hanger that I found on Amazon. I would just buy it and call it a day, unless I had the resources to make it myself.

Supplies:

- Macramé Cording: 4 mm
- Mirrored octagon
- 2 inches Wood ring
- Wood beads: 25 mm w/10 mm hole size
- Strong scissors.

Cut 4 pieces of cording macramé of 108 inches (or 3yds). Tightly and carefully pull the knots. Separate two head knots from the Lark and begin to tie them into a square knot. As you start the second knot of the square, loop it through one of the sides of the other two knots into a wide knot of the square. Fasten 7 square knots on both sides. Break the ends after the knots have been tied. Two strings per side and four in the center.

In each of the 2 side cording lines, apply one bead. Tie a knot on both sides under the bead to keep them even. Connect the four cords in the middle to a simple or (overhand knot) about 1/14 inch below the beads. Take a cord from the center and add it to the sides of the two cords. Tie the three on both sides in a knot. Apply the mirror to the end of the knot. Add one of the three sides to the mirror's back to hold it steady. Place clear knots in all 3 side cables at the bottom left and right side of the mirror. Trim the cords again on all three sides. Return one to the back of the mirror on either side and add 2 to the front of it on each side.

Flip the mirror over and tie together all the cords. Flip over the mirror and loosen the knot at the front. Inside the knot, slip the back cords and straighten the knot. Cutting the cord ends up to around 14 inches.

DIY Macramé Bag

What you're going to need

- String
- Scissors
- 2 Gold Jump Ring
- Thread and needle.

We will start by knotting the bag's strap. The length of each string piece must be half the total strap length, time 4. It is necessary that each half of the strap is knotted separately. Our straps should have been defined as a total of 45 cm, so we cut the string pieces half of that time 4. Fold the string in half and use the folded end to knot it on your hoop.

So, you make four knots, take the inner line, loop it around the outer line, and start with the knot on the right. Tighten the knot, and it should look like that. Do the knot, this time using only the string. Use the same knotting method to knot the other side of the belts, this time just reverse the direction. Do these 5 times on both sides.

Again, using the same method of knotting, by extending the knots, attach the two threads. Repeat three times these extended sets. And change direction and knot for the 3 sets from left to right. Then again repeat the side knots. You've finished half the harness once you've done this! For the other harness and hoop, do this, we will attach them. Do the same knot again to complete the knot work. Snip off one of the knot's threads, then use the strand to form a new knot. Align the ends and sew together with the needle and thread to attach the straps.

Cut 10 pieces of string four times the desired length of your bag to create the body of the rope bag. The bag we made as a guide is 15" (38 cm). Use the folded end as before to knot it onto the gold hoop. The rope bag's body is made with box knots. Starting on the side of two threads, loop it around the two middle strands. Repeat the knot and tighten the knot. Keep doing box knots till you want to have the size of the bag. Twist the end of the strings and drag a little glue into the knots to protect them if you do not want any tassel ends. Remove the bag.

CHAPTER 8:

Macramé Bracelet

Beginner's Bracelet

This is an easy Macramé project that's perfect for beginners!

What you need:

- Glue-on end clasps
- Jewelry glue
- Ring connector
- Cotton or hemp twine

Instructions:

First, take three of the hemp or cotton twine strands and make a loop out of them. Loop the loop that you have built around the connector and then make a knot on each side.

Now, you'll see 6 strands coming off the sides of your loop after you have inserted it through the connector. Braid each side—you can make simple braids, or even 6-strand braids, if you can do it.

Trim the ends off once you get to the end. Make sure to use jewelry glue and secure the braid by gluing it on. Fully twist the end caps to coat the spine of your bracelet. Check the length before securing so you can be sure that it would really fit you.

Studded Macramé Bracelet

This studded bracelet is sure to up your accessory game. It's simple but not bland. It's also regal, but definitely not overwhelming.

What you need:

- Two binder clips
- Bent nose pliers
- Needle
- Nipper tool
- Clipboard
- GS Hypo Cement
- Two 6mm/ 1.8 mm hole multi-cut rounds
- 30 4mm Sterling Silver multi-cut rounds
- 1 Swarovski Trapeze button
- 3 yards neutral leather cord
- 1 yard natural leather cord

Instructions:

Nip the ends of the leather cord so you could insert the 4mm beads.

Then, take the leather cord and slide it down the button. Make sure to center the button on the clipboard.

Center the leather cord on your 2mm cords, and then take the knotting cord over the left cord. Take the remaining part under the center and loop up to the right side. Take the right cord over the left side. Make sure to pull the cords tightly, and then let the right knotting cord pass under the center cord through the side loop. Make sure to pull both of the cords together tightly.

Clip the excess cord and leave just around ¾ of it. Make sure to center some on the cord and to wrap at least 2 mm around the cord. Slide at least three loops up, and then take the excess cord and thread it around the three loops.

To make the button hole, just make sure to pull the cord roughly until you get 1.5mm of knotting cord in your hands.

Add the Sterling multi-cut beads on the end of the leather cords and make a knot to let the embellishment sit.

Seal with hypo cement (don't worry, it's nothing like cement used for constructing houses), let dry, and use

12-Stand Spiral Bracelet

This one has quite a lot of layers to it—but it's beautiful and is something you could give away as a friendship bracelet. Now, you won't have problems looking for gifts to give away to your friends anymore!

What you need:

- Scissors
- Rattail cords (interior/exterior colors)

- Kumihino round disk
- ruler

Instructions:

Get 4 cuttings of your interior colors, and 4 cuttings of the outer color. It's up to you what colors you want to use—just make sure they complement each other. Cut the exterior color to be 45 inches long, and the interior one to be 39 inches long. Find the center of the cords as you hold them together.

Find the front of the round disk and place the center of the cords there. Lace the disk like you see on the image below.

Now, take the bottom left cord and cross it above the top left cord.

Take the bottom right cord and cross it above the top right cord.

Take the upper left cord and cross it above the bottom left cord.

Take the upper right cord and cross it above the bottom right cord.

Turn the disk, and repeat the process on the cords on the other side of the disk. You'll then notice the cords coming out of the backside.

When you feel like the length and the look of the bracelet are alright with you, go ahead and take all the cords and pinch them so they wouldn't come undone.

Take the bracelet off the disk and knot the end to close. Secure with glue and let dry before using.

Rhinestone Macramé Bracelet

This bracelet is really colorful, easy on the eyes, and is quite customizable—so it's up to you if you want to add more beads, use more colors, and the like.

What you need:

- Lighter
- Scissors
- Tape
- Embroidery needle
- 1 small rhinestone button
- 1 large rhinestone button
- 3 yards 0.8mm Chinese knitting cord

Instructions:

Cut knotting cord into 80" and 20" pieces.

Then, fold the smaller cord in half and find the center of the long cord. Make sure the center of the cord is under the two strands in the middle, and make sure it goes under the left cord.

Next, pull the cord on the left all the way to the right and middle straps so that the loop could go through to the right side. Slide the loop over the right rhinestone button.

Make continuous square knots on the left side. Repeat the steps after pulling tightly and stop knotting when you reach your desired length.

Now, get the large rhinestone button and thread it onto the 2 strands in the middle. Knot some more and add the small rhinestone button near the end, just before you close the loop.

Enjoy your new Macramé bracelet!

Lace Asymmetrical Macramé Bracelet

This one has that dainty, ladylike feel to it. For sure, you'd love wearing it on nights out with the one you love—or on Sunday brunches with family and friends!

What you need:

- Hemp twine
- Ribbons
- Small glass beads
- Glue
- Paint brush
- Water
- Knotting board

Instructions:

Cut around 60 inches of twine, and 15 inches of ribbon—and then place them on the knotting board.

While they're on the board, knot them together at the top and then mark the mid-point—around 3 ½ inches.

Thread some glass beads—it's up to you where you want them to come in, and make sure to place knots before and after you have set the beads so they would stay in place.

To keep the bracelet even more secure, you could mix water and glue together. Mix 2/3 glue with 1/3 water and then paint the back of the bracelet with it. Wipe and let dry before using.

Enjoy your new Macramé bracelet!

Intricate Lavender Macramé

Lavender is a charming color and seeing it on a Macramé bracelet is always good. This project is pretty dainty, and could really help you use your time well as it needs loads of focus!

What You Need:

- Disposable Plastic Cup
- Headpins
- Scissors
- Glue
- 26 pieces 4mm crystal bicones
- 28 pieces size 6 Color A seeds
- 26 pieces size 11 seeds
- 4 pieces rectangular 6 x 4 mm glass bugles
- 2 pieces size 6 Color B seeds
- 1 open ended circular memory wire

- C-Lon Nylon cord, divided into two: 5 ½ ft. long working cord, and 1 ft. long centerpiece cord

Instructions:

Use the disposable plastic cup to anchor the memory wire in. This way, you could prevent it from falling down as you work on your project.

Pass the middle of the working cord under the wire. Go ahead and wrap a square knot around it. Now, make sure that your two cords are already of the same length.

Then, string one of the size 6 seeds on each cord before making 2 more square knots and tying the bicord the way you tied the 6 seeds. Make sure that the knots are going in one direction and that they have uniformity.

Work enough sections until you reach the middle then add the final two beads with one square knot.

The new cord will now be your anchor so make sure that you tie it around the original cord. Repeat on the other side.

Slide the end cords in with tapestry needle and then cut and glue the shortest way you can, just to keep it secure, and aesthetically right, of course. Cut the excess cords and finally tie with an overhand knot.

CHAPTER 9:

Macramé Jewelry

Hoop Earrings

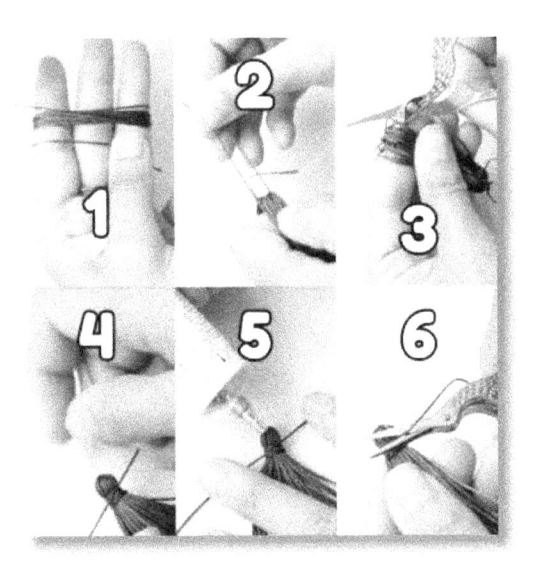

Y ou can reuse old fringes to make earrings. Many garments include fringes as decorative material that you can take advantage of to make your DIY crafts. You can find colored edges on t-shirts, bags, coats, backpacks, or bags of all kinds.

You can recycle colored fringes from clothes you no longer use. Many containers, packs, or T-shirts include these beads.

The exciting thing about making your accessories is to reuse materials and fabrics that you may have forgotten at home. In this way, you contribute to recycling, make responsible consumption, and avoid acquiring unnecessary clothing. If you have fringes, you can also buy them in jewelry bead shops.

Do you prefer to make your fringes? It is effortless, and you need synthetic and resistant thread, contact glue, and scissors.

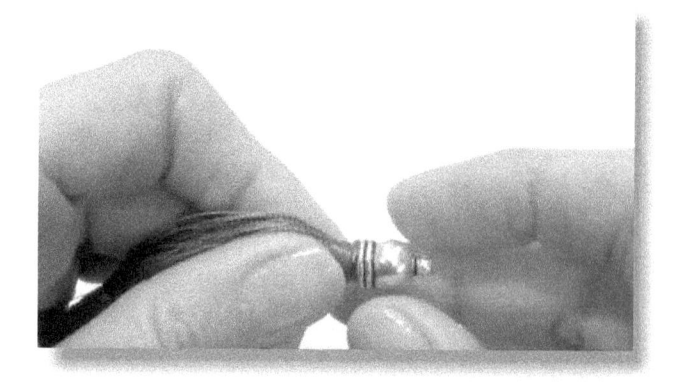

Make your fringe earrings step by step. You only need contact glue, synthetic yarn, and scissors. To complete the ornaments, you will also need jewelry caps and earring hooks. First of all, wrap 3 meters of thread over your fingers, hold it and tie it with more ribbon, cut the threads on the opposite end, use another piece of string and wrap it around the related part, tie it from behind and use glue to fix the knot. Finally, use scissors to cut the excess piece. At this point, we should already have our two fringes ready to turn them into beautiful earrings. From here, we have several options; the option that we recommend is to use jewelry caps for ornaments and contact glue. The last step is to use two earring hooks on each cap. You can use jewelry pliers if you need to open and fix the rings or any other material you use. You can get all the materials used in specialized jewelry stores or by recycling old earrings that you no longer apply.

Choker Necklace

Elegant loops allow the emerald and silver beads to stand out, making this a striking piece. The finished length is 12 inches. Be sure to use the ribbon clasp which gives multiple length options to the closure.

Knots Used:

1. Lark's Head Knot

2. Alternating Lark's Head Chain

Supplies:

- 3 strands of black C-Lon cord; two 7ft cords, one 4ft cord

- 18 - green beads (4mm)

- 7 - round silver beads (10 mm)

- Fasteners: Ribbon Clasps, silver

- Glue - Beacon 527 multi-use

- Note: Bead size can vary slightly. Just be sure all beads you choose will slide onto 2 cords.

Instructions:

1. Optional – Find the center of your cord and attach it to the top of the ribbon clasp with a lark's head knot. I found it easier to thread the loose ends through and pull them down until my loop was near the opening, then push the cords through the loop. Repeat with the 2 remaining strands, putting the four-foot cord in the center. If this is problematic, you could cut all the cords to 7ft and not worry about placement. (If you really trust your glue, you

can skip this step by gluing the cords into the clasp and going from there).

2. Lay all cords into the ribbon clasp. Add a generous dap of glue and use pliers to close the clasp.

MACREMe' FOR BEGINNERS

3. You now have 6 cords to work with. Find the 4 ft. cords and place them in the center. They will be the holding (or filler) cords throughout.

4. Begin your Alternating Lark's Head (ALH) chain, using the outmost right cord then the outermost left cord. Follow with the other right cord then the last left cord. For this first set, the pattern will be hard to see. You may need to tug gently on the cords to get a little slack in them.

93 | Pag.

5. Now slide a silver bead onto the center 2 cords.

6. The outer cords are now staggered on your holding cords. Continue with the ALH chain by knotting with the upper right cord then tie a knot with the top left cord.

7. Finish your set of 4 knots, then add a green bead

8. Tie four ALH knots followed by a green bead until you have 3 green beads in the pattern. Then tie one more set of 4 ALH knots.

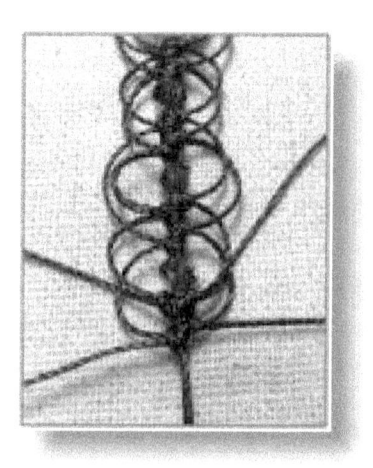

9. Slide on a silver bead and continue creating sequences of 3 green, 1 silver (always with 4 ALH knots between each). End with the 7th silver bead and 1 more set of 4 ALH knots, for a 12" necklace. (Use this to shorten or lengthen as you choose).

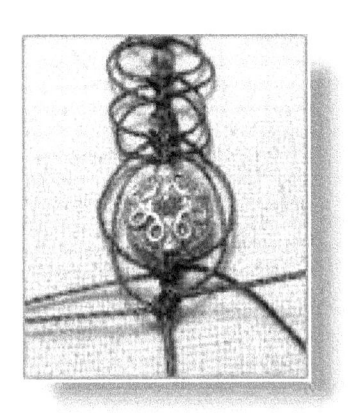

10. Lay all cords in the ribbon clasp and glue well.

11. Crimp shut and let dry completely. Trim excess cords.

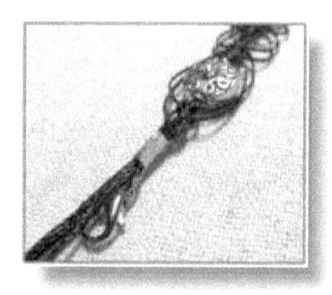

Serenity Bracelet

(Note: if you are familiar with the flat knot, you can move right along into the pattern)

This novice bracelet offers plenty of practice using one of micro macramé's most used knots. You will also gain experience beading and equalizing tension. This bracelet features a button closure and the finished length is 7 inches.

Knots Used:

Flat Knot (aka square knot)

Overhand knot

Supplies:

- White C-Lon cord, 6 ½ ft., x 3
- 18 - Frosted Purple size 6 beads
- 36 - Purple seed beads, size 11
- 1 - 1 cm Purple and white focal bead
- 26 - Dark Purple size 6 beads
- 1 - 5 mm Purple button closure bead

(Note: the button bead needs to be able to fit onto all 6 cords)

Instructions:

1. Take all 3 cords and fold them in half. Find the center and place on your work surface as shown:

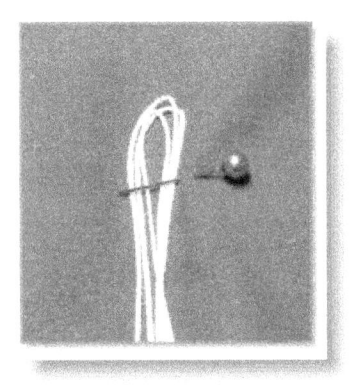

2. Now hold the cords and tie an overhand knot, loosely, at the center point. It should look like this:

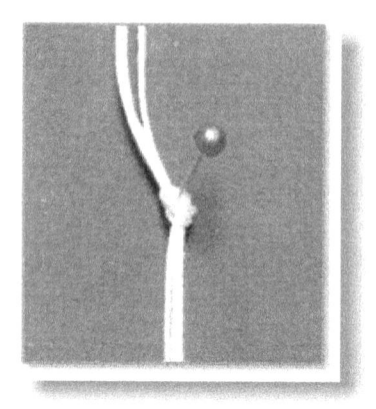

3. We will now make a buttonhole closure. Just below the knot, take each outer cord and tie a flat knot (aka square knot). Continue tying flat knots until you have about 2 ½ cm.

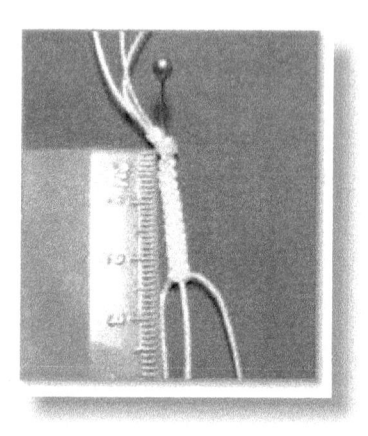

4. Undo your overhand knot and place the ends together in a horseshoe shape.

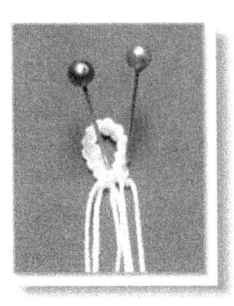

5. We now have all 6 cords together. Think of the cords as numbered 1 through 6 from left to right. Cords 2-5 will stay in the middle as filler cords. Find cord 1 and 6 and use these to tie flat knots around the filler cords. (Note: now you can pass your button bead through the opening to ensure a good fit. Add or subtract flat knots as needed to create a snug fit. This size should be fine for a 5mm bead). Continue to tie flat knots until you have 4 cm worth. (To increase bracelet length, add more flat knots here, and the equal amount in step 10).

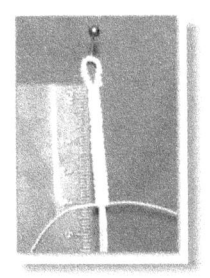

6. 4. Separate cords 1-4-1. Find the center 2 cords. Thread a size 6 frosted purple bead onto them, then tie a flat knot with cords 2 and 5.

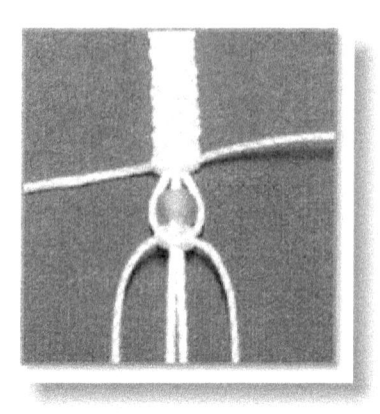

7. 5. We will now work with cords 1 and 6. With cord 1, thread on a seed bead, a dark purple size 6 bead and another seed bead. Repeat with cord 6, then separate the cords into 3-3. Tie a flat knot with the left 3 cords. Tie a flat knot with the right 3 cords.

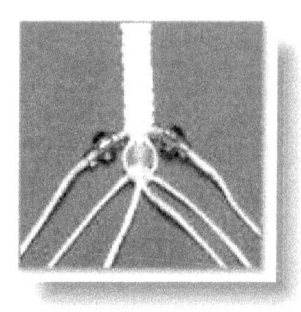

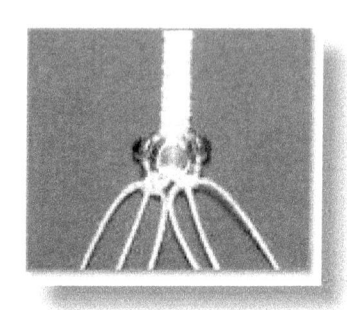

8. 6. Repeat step 4 and 5 three times.

9. Find the center 2 cords, hold together and thread on the 1cm focal bead. Take the cords out (2 and 5) and bead as follows: 2 size 6 dark purple beads, a frosted purple bead, and 2 dark purple beads. Find cords 1 and 6 and bead as follows: 2 frosted purple beads, a seed bead, a dark purple bead, a seed bead, 2 frosted purple beads.

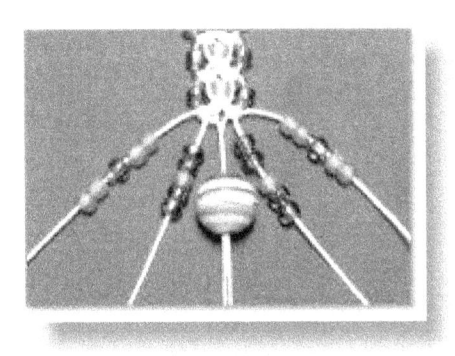

3. With cords 2 and 5, tie a flat knot around the center 2 cords. Place the center 4 cords together and tie a flat knot around them with outer cords 1 and 6.

4. Repeat steps 4 and 5 four times.

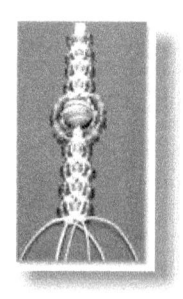

5. Repeat step 3.

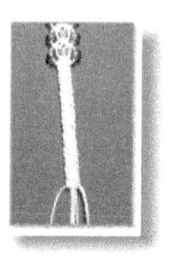

6. Place your button bead on all 6 cords and tie an overhand knot tight against the bead. Glue well and trim the cords.

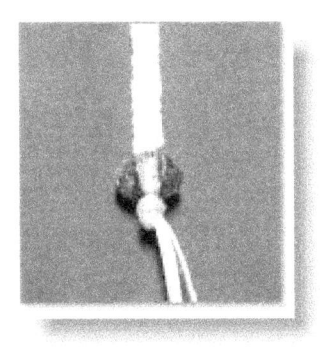

Lantern Bracelet

This pattern may look simply, but please don't try it if you are in a hurry. This one takes patience. Don't worry about getting your picot knots all the exact same shape. Have fun with it! The finished bracelet is 7 ¼ inches in length. If desired, add a picot knot and a spiral knot on each side of the center piece to lengthen it. This pattern has a jump ring closure.

Knots Used: Lark's Head Knot Spiral Knot Picot Knot Overhand Knot

Supplies:

- 3 strands of C-Lon cord (2 light brown and 1 medium brown) 63-inch lengths
- Fasteners (1 jump ring, 1 spring ring or lobster clasp)
- Glue - Beacon 527 multi-use
- 8 small beads (about 4mm) amber to gold colors
- 30 gold seed beads
- 3 beads (about 6 mm) amber color (mine are rectangular, but round or oval will work wonderfully also)
- Note: Bead size can vary slightly. Just be sure all beads you choose will slide onto 2 cords (except seed beads).

Instructions:

1. Find the center of your cord and attach it to the jump ring with a lark's head knot. Repeat with the 2 remaining strands. If you want the 2-tone effect, be sure your second color is NOT placed in the center, or it will only be a filler cord and you will end up with a 1 tone bracelet.

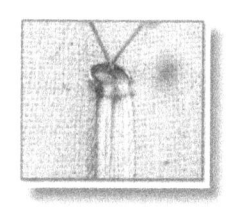

2. You now have 6 cords to work with. Think of them as numbered 1 thorough 6, from left to right. Move cords 1 and 6 apart from the rest. You will use these to work the spiral knot. All others are filler cords. Take cord number 1 tie a spiral knot. Always begin with the left cord. Tie 7 more spirals.

3. Place a 4mm bead on the center 2 cords. Leave cords 1 and 6 alone for now and work 1 flat knot using cords 2 and 5.

4. Now put cords 2 and 5 together with the center strands. Use 1 and 6 to tie a picot flat knot. Gently tug the cords into place then lock in tightly with the spiral knot.

Notice here how I am holding the picot knot with my thumbs while pulling the cords tight with my fingers.

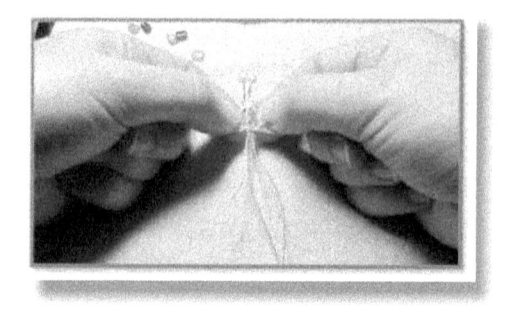

5. Tie 8 spiral knots (using left cord throughout pattern).

6. Place a 4mm bead on the center 2 cords. Leave cords 1 and 6 alone for now and work 1 flat knot using cords 2 and 5. Now put cords 2 and 5 together with the center strands. Use strands 1 and 6 to tie a picot flat knot.

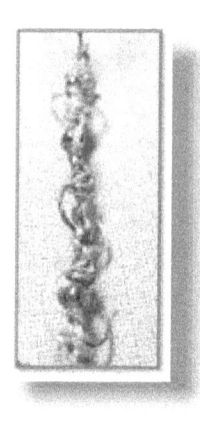

8. Place 5 seed beads on cords 1 and 6. Put cords 3 and 4 together and string on a 6 mm bead. Tie one flat knot with the outermost cords.

Repeat this step two more times.

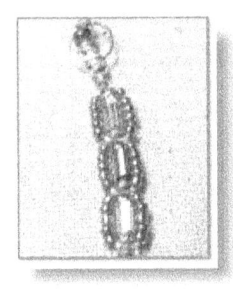

Thread on your clasp. Tie an overhand knot with each cord and glue well. Let dry completely. As this is the weakest point in the design, I advise trimming the excess cords and gluing again. Let dry.

Macramé Earrings are great because they're definitely not like your usual boring, silver or gold earrings. From neon ones to the more subdued and elegant, you'll surely find the right Macramé Earrings for you!

CHAPTER 10:

Indoor Project Ideas

There's an infinite range of ways to practice a new talent or art, much like everything in existence. I'm not going to pretend I'm a macramé specialist. I'm a complete newbie, really. I'm actually going to guide you on my unique experience from one beginner to another and teach you one way to do things.

The best thing is you don't need to be a specialist in making beautifully stunning items of furniture for your house. Honestly, it looks a lot harder than it is. Let's get to it, then.

Retro Styles To Show Macramé In House

A Trend from the past to the blast

Macramé has seen its flash in the fame through many times of history. When many people imagine such twisted bits of art, they always look back to the time when it hit the highest point of joy — the seventies, when the craze became all -bohemian-things.

Yet its success predated hundreds of years until the age of grooviness and bell-bottoms. It was initially of all the fashion of Arab Weavers of the 13th century. In the 17th century, Queen Mary applied this to the UK. Later, in the Victorian period, the weaving method saw another resurgence, emerging as simple, knotted patterns on lacy designs, nearly 100 years until it appeared again in the 1970s.

And now it's again back, and maybe due to creative artisans and designers, it's better than ever. When the patterns in decoration move to boho specifics and quirky style, there has been a gradual evolution to taking back macramé.

If you haven't hopped aboard the new-day macramé ship, you might picture the crumbling owl with descend eyes hanging for decades in the corner of the house of your mother. Although those macramé items can actually be right in vintage-inspired spaces, fresh, today's patterns marry the new and the old, using inventively old ideas.

In order to stay faithful to the previous essence of macramé, although adopting them in the 21st century, below are few inspirations for the designs to get you going.

Fiber Art

When viewed as a futuristic interpretation of the dream catcher, Macramé's artwork gives a change into current times. Hoops and soft macramé create works of art ideal for the daily. Dream catchers are usually placed over the bunk, a place where items like this will feel right at home.

Plant Hangers

It gets no more classic macramé than a hanger to a tomato. There's no denying that your mom had some sort of hanging in your house as you grew up. Now those plants are trendy again, and also leafy greens cover on-trend location, macramé plant hangers give any sense, particularly those hangers with twisted, subtle detailing. For the perfect Instagram-ready setting, hang yours along with walls.

Wall Hangings

The wall hangings appear to be the norm when it's about macramé. Do you choose lightweight or strong weaving? Long or short? Dip-dyed or white? And nowadays, only macramé wall art can be ordered that suspended from a recycled part of driftwood. They are flexible and can suit virtually everywhere in the house, including a pint-sized wall that requires anything to cover it or a room where it could be contrasted with framed photos.

Votive Holders

How's that creative? Small glass jars dressing up to make their own macramé. The weavings give to the candle holders a touch of coziness, where they can be viewed on a nightstand, a bath counter, or even an outdoor patio.

Patterned Stools

Macramé often makes a beautiful addition to a bench or chair, each of two as a decorative decoration, or as a nice place to relax, whether the yarns are durable. Be that as it might, it may look cute placed in a corner between decorative items and plant, or show many over a dining table.

Woven Hammocks

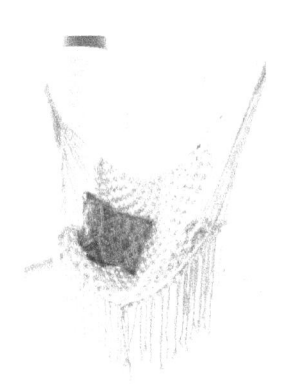

Yeah, in a backyard will be the throwback place to view a macramé hammock, but we think it fits much better inside. Hang it in a corner to act as a laid-back reading nook or on a three-season porch where you can enjoy Netflix and soak in the outdoor scenery.

Knit Placemats

Making your house appear as if by showing macramé placemats or a runner on your dining room table, it sprang from the pages of an Anthropology catalog. Macramé functions for a wide range of tables capes, from boho to beach and most of all. It conveys a calm and modeled environment.

Decorative Garlands

It is no accident that a macramé garland might possibly act as a belt might have been carried by Stevie Nicks in the '70s. Alternatively, place yours at this, above your bed or fence, or around a windowsill, on such a wall hanger.

Door Curtains

This isn't almost as loud as the string curtains of the 70s. Hang a floating macramé curtain for a touch of dreaminess to attach to every doorway.

Hanging Chandeliers

Bring a chandelier made in macramé into your decor for a glimpse of a flower-child. You may either hang it as a discussion piece of its own, or others have the option to bring an LED light into the room, projecting a magical glow throughout. Yeah, macramé is definitely the hour's fashion theme, so we don't know how long it's going to hang around this period, so let's enjoy it while here.

Make a Fabric Coil Bowl

Attach a neon flash with those woven coil bowls to your desk or shelves. They will also make a beautiful homemade present, maybe a small bowl with a few wash tapes rolls inside? ... Not much until Christmas

What You Will Need:

Long fabric strips – everything will work: I used both cotton and acrylic knits. The blue neon in a discount bin was the dirt-cheap yard, and the gray lines were Spaghetti thread. You may also use pieces of clothing, recycled T-shirts, or thrifted fabrics and tablecloths.

Cord – the fluorescent orange from the hardware store is 'Brickie's Side' ($5 per 100 meters) – and you can use more fabric or yarn as I did for the pink cups. You'll use the best of this. For the gray bowl, I used about 8 – 10 meters (about 8.5 – 11 yards), and it's around 14 cm (5.5 inches) long x 8 cm (3.5 inches) thick. The number seen in the picture below is not a true representation.

A large needle in the thread with a wide head.

Scissors.

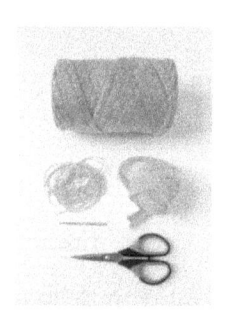

If you cut fabric (T tops, mats, cotton yard, etc.), the thicker, the chunkier you cut it, and the smaller the bowl would be. A decent size for tiny bowls is around 3.5 cm (1.5) "long. The illustration below shows how one piece of fabric may be sliced into a continuous row if you cut the fabric to extend it at a time in tiny pieces and the fabric coils into a comfortable circular 'yarn' shape.

The instructional pictures are of neon orange stitching for the gray pot, so from now on, I'll stick to those shades. Let's continue ... Cut the length of an orange cord as far as you can without it being twisted, then loop it with the needle. Mine was around 2 meters (just below 2 meters).

To get a decent thickness, I used three bits of grey cotton yarn together. I cut it down to around 1.4 meters (4.5 ft.) wide. If you choose one layer of the yarn, it doesn't need to be sliced; it may sit on the ball/spool. Your thread length would differ on whether you want to alter colors. However, it's all pretty free style-you can't make errors!

Overlap the orange cord ends and grey yarn as well—four to Five times Loop the string around the thread.

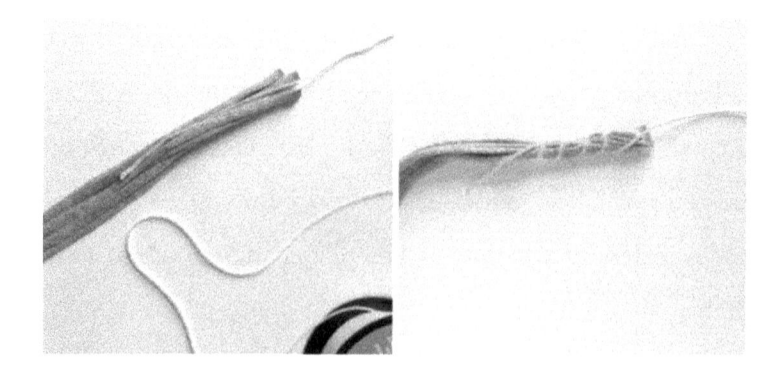

Fold the grey yarn end over to create a circle. Keep the hole as tiny as you can in the middle – it will be only wide enough to go through the needle because it should become wider when you stitch across the yarn. Wrap the cord around the yarn loop center, let a short tail stick out, and tie a knot. (As in the screenshot to the left below). Keep the yarn as seen on top of the short tail and on the bottom of the long piece of yarn.

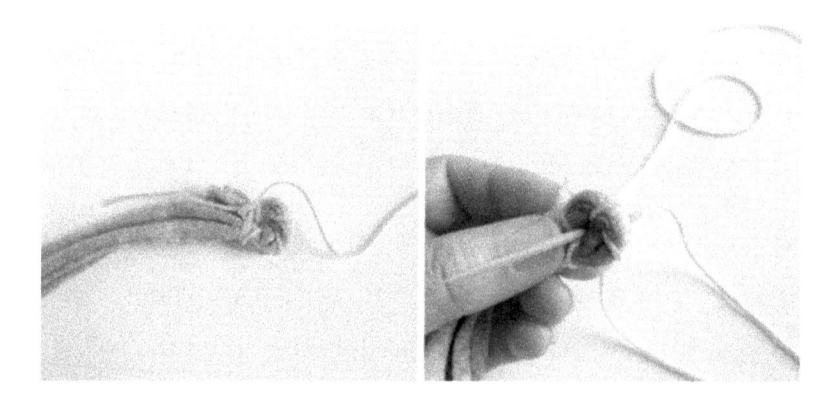

Do not knot the rope-leaving a rope at the top (as seen in the photo below).

Then pass through the loop, through the needle, much like a thread on a scarf.

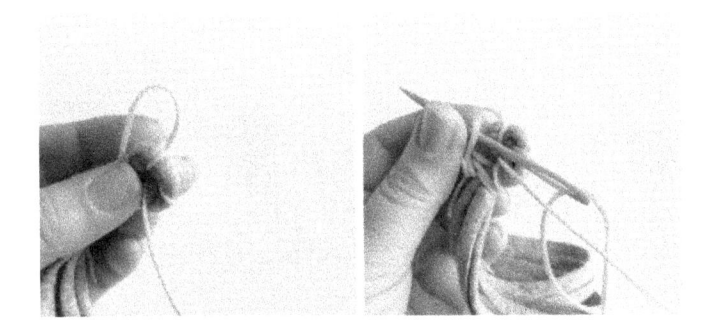

Repeat the stitch around the loop all the way. Needle in from back to front through the opening. Leave a thread, and pass into it the pin. Push closed knot. The stitch should be strong but not heavy. Hold the stitches tight together and move around (like in the picture below on the right hand).

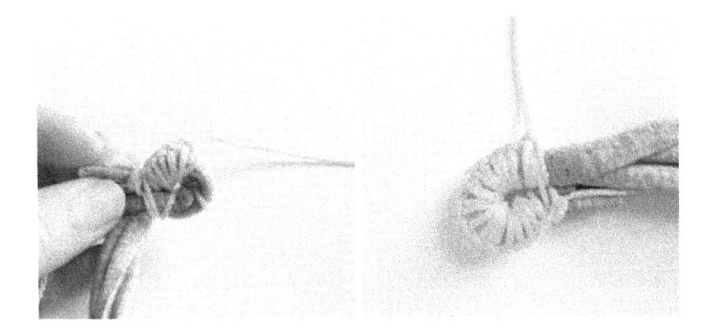

Fold over the orange cord's starting tail and the gray yarn's short tail on top with the long gray yarn (left-hand picture below). Your next stitch would go through your first blanket stitch in the back rather than through the opening. Bring the needle out to the back of the first blanket stitch and put it around the edges. The next stitch passes across the top of the second stitch on the scarf. Move down to the next picture for a closer peek at where the arrow moves.

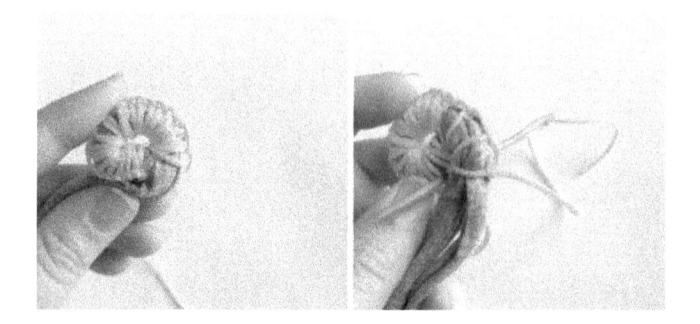

You've done a lot of stitching, and you possibly would quickly run out of thread. The photo below to the right illustrates how to attach a new cord duration. Knot the two parts together, such that the knot is on the coil's edge.

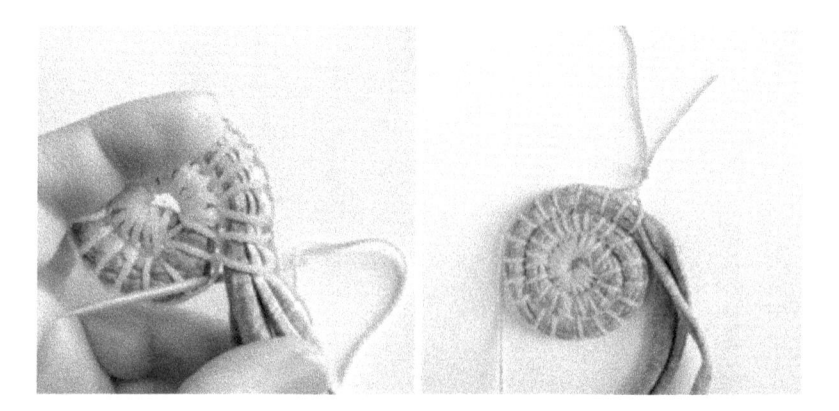

Race the tails over the grey thread and tuck them in with the knot while you start stitching (see image below left). I sometimes inserted an additional stitch when my coil expanded as I felt they were growing too far away. Recall not drawing the stitches so close, so the bowl's foundation won't sit level.

What you have to do is combine the old with the fresh as you run out of colors or decide to swap colors. I cut everyone a different length because I used three strands of yarn and put the fresh ones in the center of them, and there wouldn't be bulk all in one spot.

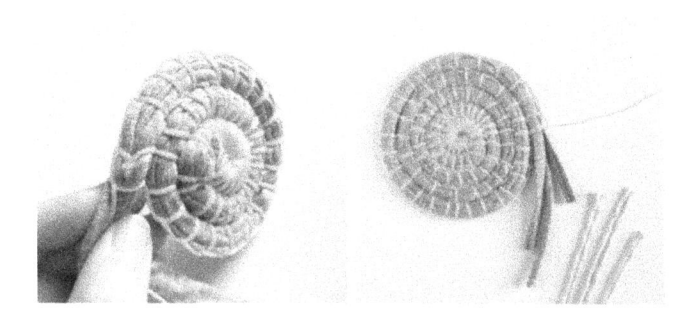

As the thread of fabric appears to curl up, I open up every piece and put the fresh one into it. So just keep on sewing.

When you are happy with the base size, you will start to build up the sides. Give the stitches a little firmer when keeping the thread above, instead of next to the previous coil. Go on like this until the target height is achieved.

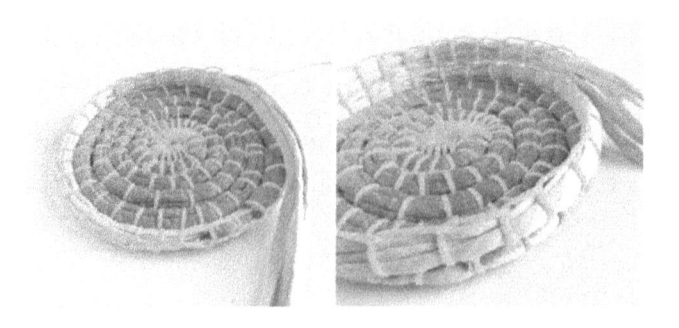

Moving off. If more than one strand of yarn is used to split them at spaced lengths to reduce the weight, continue to stitch around until there's only one strand remaining. Left on 10 cm (4 inches) of the tail, and you've got ample research to do.

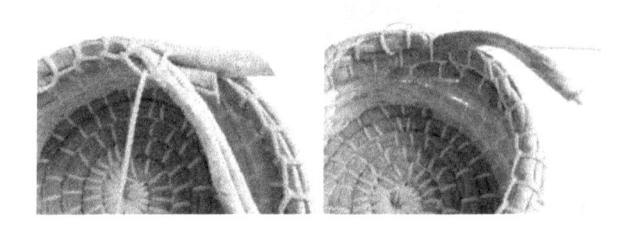

Weave the tails into one of the vertical stitches (on the inside of the bowl) below the lines. Then thread in with a couple more stitches in that row and cut off the yarn, so the tail doesn't stand out (picture below on the left).

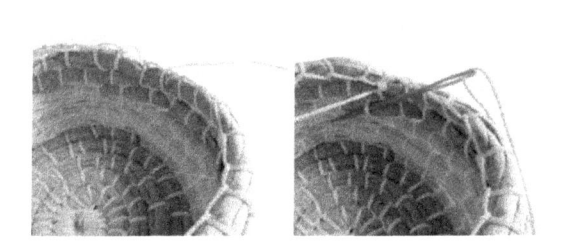

CHAPTER 11:

Macramé Candle Holder

1. You need: thread in cotton, empty container, and scissors

2. Break long cord around the container, which you must attach (cord A). I cut cord 40 cm in length for my idea.

3. Split lengthy cables (cord B). Knotting makes the job even shorter, just quick enough to sever the cords. My container has a height of 13 cm. I cut out 56 single cords-45 cm long each. I divided them into two and ended with 112 cords. Remember: You must combine the cords into a set of 4 cords. In this design, every knot is made of 4 cords. I have 112 cords in my house, with 28 groups of four cords.

4. Larks knots in the Back. We must use Larks Knots to fasten all cords B to A one's.

Half Fold cord B and put cord A under it. Pull cord B tails via loop (see picture). Tight pull. Echo on the other B-cords.

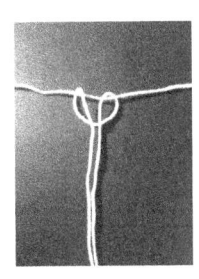

5. I attached ends of cord A to 2 keys in my desk drovers to make my job simpler. You may use a chair, for example.

I knotted the head-knot of 56 larks. That brings 112 cords.

6. Knot Square. We'll launch our square knots pattern with sennit. Make a cord A and split ends around the basin. To make a square knot, take (1, 2, 3, 4) four cords: a) put the right one (4th one) towards the left below

the two centered cords (2nd & 3rd) and the left cord (1st one). Put the left cord (1) above the two center cords (2, 3) to the right, and below the right chord. Pull both the left and right cords (1st and 4th one) to connect the knot firmly.

B) put the right (4th one) cord towards the left above the two center (2, 3) cords and below the left (1st) chord. Place the left one below two center cords (2nd & 3rd) to the right, then above the right cord (4th one). Stretch cords right and left to secure your knot (1, 2).

7. Make three square knots of sennit on every 4-cord ring. (Sennit-knot links, bound one after the other)

8. Stretch 4. Triangles-ties alternate in line. To make triangles, split the cords into different pairs. To build four reversed triangles, I split my 112 cords by 28. Using the alternative square knots to create a triangle-pick two right strings (3rd & 4th one) from one sennite and two of the left cords (1st & 2nd) from the next sennite and make knot squares.

For my triangle development project, I made: Row four to seven alternative square knots, Row five to six alternative square knots, Row six to five alternative square knots, Row seven to row four alternative square knots, Row eight to 3rd row, alternative square knots, Row nine to row 2nd alternative square knots, Row ten to row 1st alternative square knots. I produced a further three triangles using the same pattern.

Note: If you have a specific amount of cords, you can do some maths. For e.g., you can combine them into 25 4-cord combines if you have 100 cords, and create five triangles (each triangle would have 20 cords= five alternating square knots). You can divide them into 30 4-cord sets if you have 120 cords, and create six triangles (each triangle would have 20 cords = 5 alternating square knots).

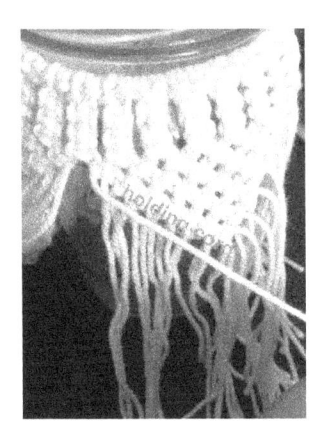

9. Take the extreme-left rope (holding rope) from the 1st left alternative square knot and positioned it above all other working cords diagonally. Take a functioning cord far left and create a counter-clockwise loop around the holding cord. Stretch securely on the functioning thread. Repeat to finish the dual half-hitch from the same cords. For all other operating cords, start double half hook. Thread 2 of the final alternating square knot (on top of the inverted triangle) is the only functioning thread.

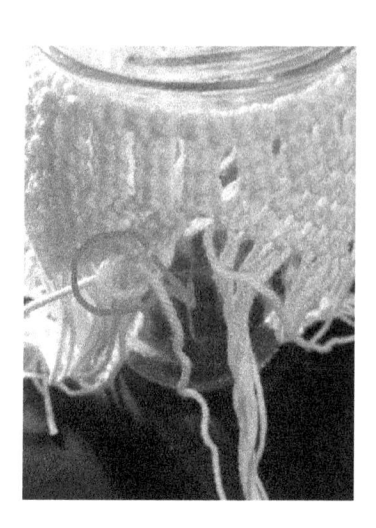

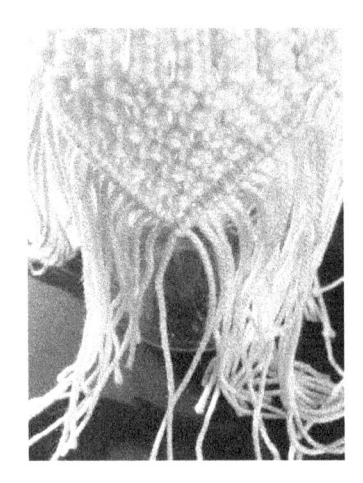

B) From right side to left side: Grab the extreme-right rope (holding rope) from the final right alternative square knot and position it above all other working cords diagonally (to the left). Take a functioning cord far-right and create a circle around the holding cord in a clockwise direction. Stretch securely on the functioning thread. Repeat to finish the dual half-hitch from the same cords. For all other operating cords, start double half hook.

Take the left cord and right cord to finish the arrangement, and render clockwise double half hook.

10. Cut both strings to ends.

Macramé Fiber Garland:

Things you're going to need:

- Thread
- Painters tape
- Scissors

- Image nails
- A clip to enjoy while you tie knots.

Stage 1: Cut the important part of the yarn to the width you like. I cut these ones to 75 inches, by having in mind that 1 I would need around 5 inches for hanging on either end and 2) draping it will strip away most of its' breadth until I had installed the garland.

Stage 2: Cut any single yarn pieces. I split my important part of yarn for 1.5 to see how much total yarn cuts I will like, as I needed about 1.5" apart for every product. I had in mind the colors that I needed to be highlights and the colors that I wanted to show more and split the cuts appropriately. I split every single piece to around 36" long to give plenty of space for failure, which was perfect because I made some mistakes.

Step 3: Use tape for the painters to tape your main yarn piece. In your chosen order, add your fiber cuttings by making a single knot over the central part of the yarn. True talk: if you're saying, "Oh, this looks amazing already, and I don't feel saying making a lot of knots about few next hours," I'm not going to criticize. This is pretty good for me.

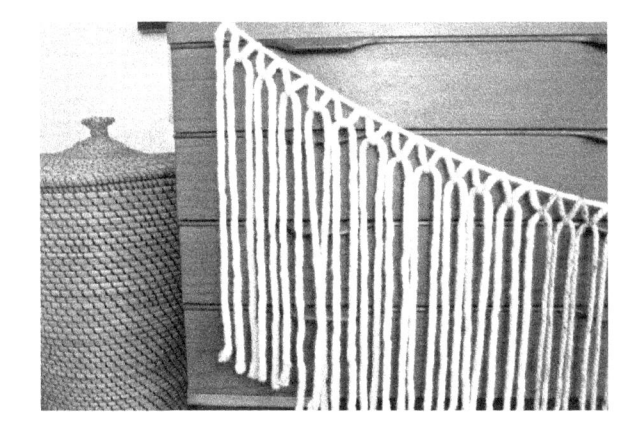

Step 4: I couldn't do anything else, so I pushed forward. Tap the highest bit of yarn on the bottom left. Make a double knot in between the second and third yarn bits. I spaced my knots around 1 inch apart, but you might spread them further apart if you need a great transparent feel. Move on until you hit the correct leg.

Step 5: Switch to the left side after you finish the first sequence, and begin again. Begin this time, on the far left with the initial piece of yarn. Again, bind double knots along this line before you get to the top.

Step 6-Another band! Miss the first bit of yarn once again this time. Start by joining the third and second part of yarn with a double knot, then push all towards the right.

Step 7: Cut the tails evenly, but don't be just like me. (Don't worry, the Windex took care of this.) As long as the yarn was still adorned, I trimmed them and resulted up with non-similar ends that I didn't understand until I put it back in my bedroom. I will recommend that you hang it straight over, and you can get a clear understanding of how both the tails are that's what I made at the end.

Step 8: Put up the wall ish! I used a small nail at either end and then wrapped the thread across the nails.

CHAPTER 12:

How to Make Your Own Macramé Designs

DIY Tassel and Macramé Key Chains

Who doesn't love a sweet ring? Particularly a lovely DIY version which takes no time to make, uses stuff you've already got, can be as simple or as fantastic as you want? If you need an excuse to make a personalized keychain, we have you:

Update your keychain before remembering it, create a replacement set of keys for your domestic pet sitter, make a replacement set of keys you can leave from your neighbor so that when you lockout you have not to break into your own place.

- Materials needed for Macramé Key chains
- Key Ring
- 3/16" Natural Cotton Piping Cord
- Beads
- Embroidery yarn or floss
- Scissors

You can make things fancy on your key chains tassel or macramé by wrapping them in different yarn or floss colors.

DIY Round Macramé Boho Coasters

I don't seem to be able to rest every time I find a craft idea, until I know how to do that, these coasters are the perfect example, I've done a macramé bracelet before, but to make a macramé round is strange for me. After exploring the internet, finding some confusing posts, and making my first coaster after ways to create it. That's the way I found it easier (although there's another one I tested as well) and it also got me the most beautiful result.

Supplies:

- 3 mm cotton cord
- Something to hold the cords, a cork coaster or a board, either tape or as I used it.
- Pins to hold if the cork is used.
- Fabric Scissors
- Ruler or measuring tape
- Comb

Boho Christmas Trees

Cut the yarn in 7-8-inch bits. Take two strands and fold them in half in order to form a loop. Place one of the loops under a twig. Start with the bowed end of the other strand and move the ends of the strand under the twig through the loop. Thread through the loop below the twig the ends of that strand. Pull tightly and repeat, okay? If you have added enough knotted strands, use a brush or a comb to separate the threads.

The "almost finished" tree is going to be a little floppy so you have to stiffen it with some starch.

When erect, cut the Boho Christmas trees into a triangle shape and decorate them with small baubles or beads. I just made the jewelry wire a little flower star. They're going to take about 10 minutes to make a whole bunch. I think they'd make beautiful gifts, or you could hang them on your Christmas tree.

Friendship Bracelet Watch

You'll need your watch face and floss to get started. I use art floss in the colors of brown, white and minty blue. Cut strips approximately 48 inches long. You will need 10 of these long strands for each side for this watch face (but just cut 10 right now, leave the others until you're ready to start from the other side). To start making our harness, we will lash each piece of floss onto the chain. Bring together the ends of a long piece of floss and pick up the end. Push through the bar and pull the ends through the loop you've built. Start with all your floss cutting. Make sure you keep the colors in your pattern as you want them. I wanted thick orange and mint stripes and thin white stripes. My order was, therefore: orange, orange, white, mint, mint, mint, mint, mint, and white, orange, orange.

And now you're just starting to braid your friendship. We won't have this weird thing bundled up in most friendship bracelets that begins with a knot, because we've latched on the message. Pretty better, huh? You have the choice, like any other friendship bracelet, to twist and then tie when you are wearing it. This is not the most beautiful option, but it's going to work well. But if you want to use closures, continue reading.

You want to take a decent amount of glue when you get the length and run a line where you need to cut. Apply the glue on the front and back sides of the threads. This will hold the braid securely together. I used the fast-dry tacky glue from Aleena because I'm very impatient. I didn't think about this and I had to shorten my straps after a few wears. Perhaps you'd like to go ahead and make the watch a bit tight. The first wear may be uncomfortable, but it will be perfect for a couple of hours. Use sharp scissors to cut the area where you applied the glue through your strap. See how well it sticks with each other?

Go ahead and run a little at the very end to help avoid fraying. Place the clamp on the end of the straps and use the pin to lock on firmly. Finish with a jumping ring on one and a jumping ring and closing on the other.

And you got it there! It's a pretty fun wear watch and brings in a new way the whole trend of the friendship bracelet.

What do you think about it? Are you going to make one? It sounds like a great project for me on the weekend!

Rainbows might appear childish to your teenagers, yet this rainbow wall dangling from Lia Griffith is tasteful enough to be equally whimsical and mature.

This DIY project would appear charming in a childhood bedroom or living area and may be customized with distinctive colors.

Take a look at the tutorial to get extra info.

Macramé Charm and Feather Décor

Charms and feathers always look cool. They just add a lot of that enchanting feeling to your house and knowing that you could make Macramé décor with charms and feathers really take your crafting game to new heights! Check out the instructions below and try it out for yourself!

What you need:

Stick/dowel

Feathers and charms with holes (for you to insert the thread in)

Embroidery/laundry rope (or any other rope or thread that you want)

Instructions:

Around 10 to 12 pieces is good, and then fold each in half. Make sure to create a loop at each end, like the ones you see below:

Then, go and loop each piece of thread on the stick.

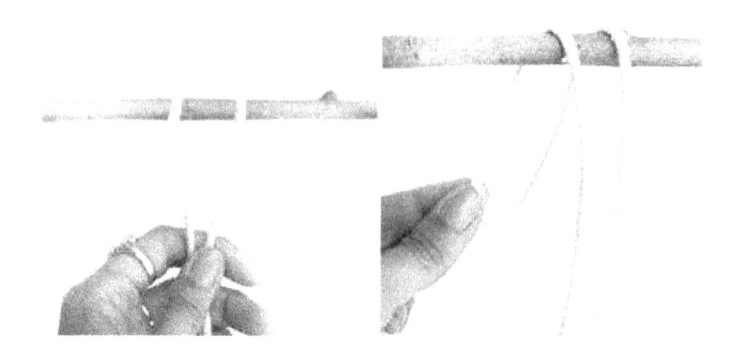

Make use of the square knot and make sure you have four strands for each knot. Let the leftmost strand cross the two strands and then put it over the strands that you have in the middle. Tuck it under the middle two, as well.

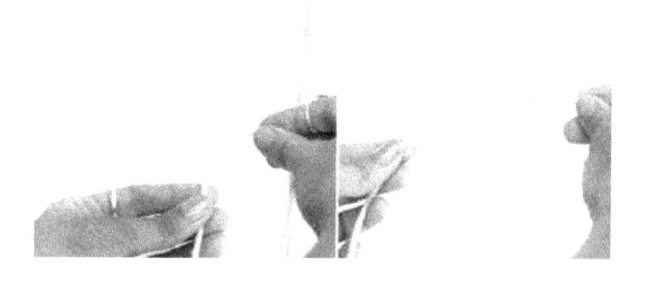

Check under the strands and let the rightmost strand be tucked under the loop to the left-hand strand.

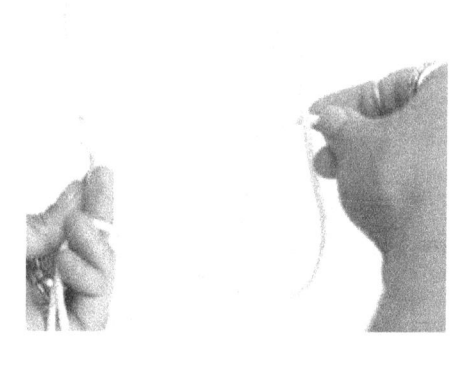

Tighten the loop by pulling the outer strands together and start with the left to repeat the process on the four strands. You will then see that a square knot has formed after tightening the loops together.

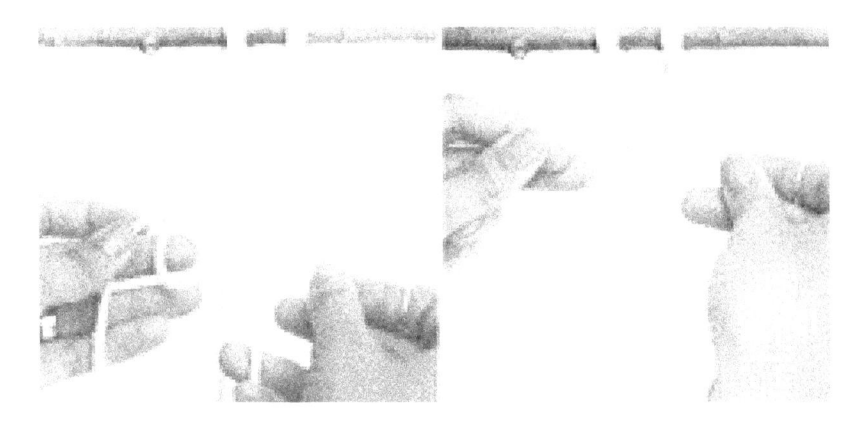

Connect the strands together by doing square knots with the remaining four pieces of rope and then repeat the process again from the left side. Tighten the loop by pulling the outer strands together and start with the left to repeat the process on the four strands. You will then see that a square knot has formed after loops have been tightened together.

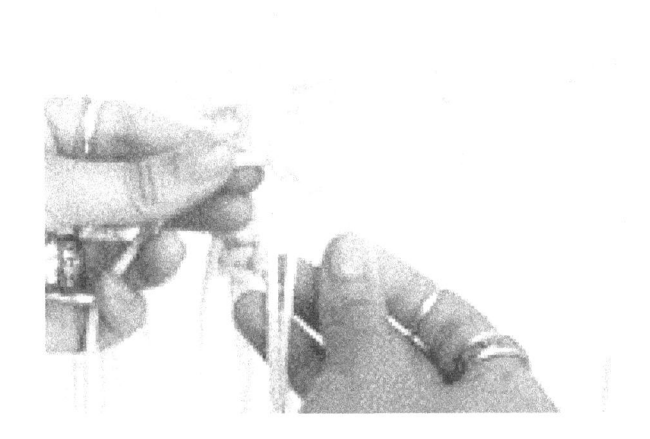

You can then do an eight knot and then just attach charms and feathers to the end. Glue them in and burn the ends for better effect!

Wreath of Nature

Just imagine having a Macramé wreath in your home! This one is inspired by nature and is one of the most creative things you could do with your time!

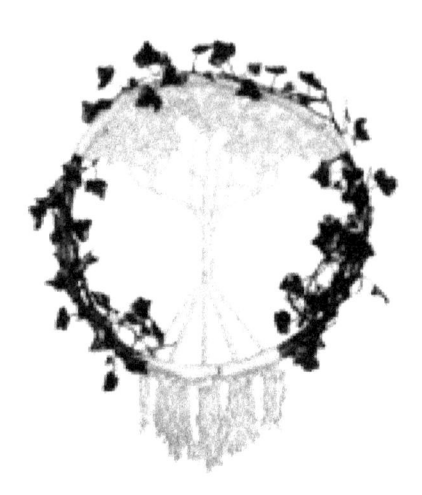

What you need:

- Clips or tape
- Fabric glue
- Wreath or ring frame
- 80 yards 12" cords
- 160 yards 17-18" cords
- 140 yards 14-16" cords
- 120 yards 12-13" cords

Instructions:

Mount the cords on top of the wreath and make the crown knot by folding one of the cords in half. Let the cords pass through the ring and then fold a knot and make sure to place it in front of the ring. Let the loops go over the ring and pull them your way so they could pass the area that has been folded.

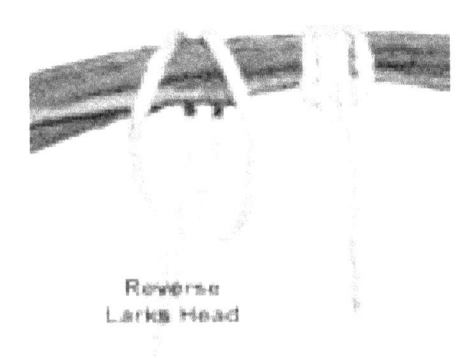

Reverse Larks Head

Let the ends pass over the first loop so you could make way for some half-hitches. Let them go over and under the ring, and then tightly pull it over the cord. This way, you'd get something like the one below. Repeat these first few steps until you have mounted all the cords on top of the ring. Organize them in groups of ten.

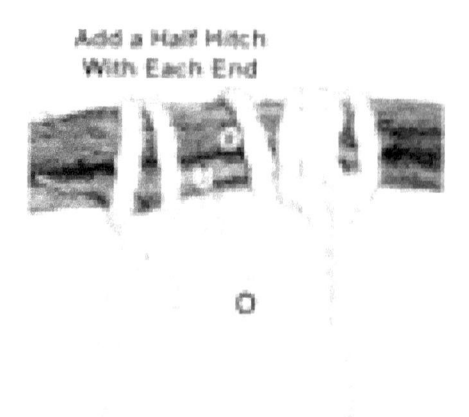

Now, you can make leaf-like patterns. To do this, make sure to number the first group of cords on the right side and make half-hitches in a counterclockwise direction. Take note that you have to place the holding plate horizontally. If you see that it has curved slightly, make sure to reposition it and then attach cords labeled 5 to 7. Move it to resemble a diagonal position and then attach cords 8 to 10.

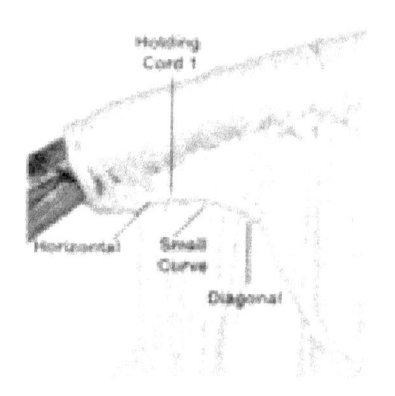

Make sure knots have been pushed close together and then use the cord on the leftmost corner to lower the leaf-like portion. The first four cords should be together on the handle and then go and attach cords labeled 3 to 6 to the holding cord. Move the cords so they'd be in a horizontal position.

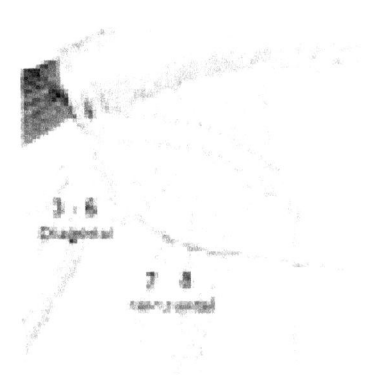

Now, move the cord upwards so that the center would not curve unnecessarily. Repeat the process for the cords on the bottom part of the frame and then start making the branches by selecting 2 to 4 cords from each of the leaves. Don't select the first and second row's first and last leaves.

Hold the cords with tape or clips as you move them towards the back of the design and decide how you want to separate—or keep the branches together. Secure the cords with glue after moving them to the back.

Wrap the right cords around the ones on the left so that branches could be joined together. Make sure to use half-hitches to wrap this portion and then use a set of two cords to create a branch.

Together with your wrap, make use of another wrap and make sure they all come together as one.

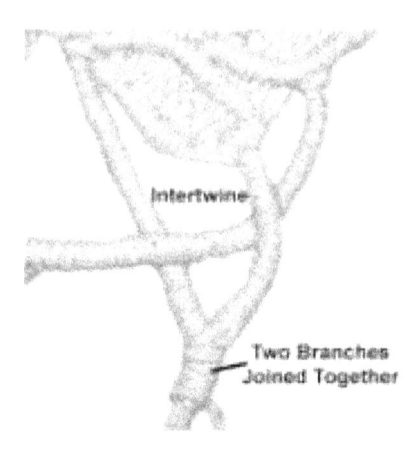

Secure the bundle by wrapping a 3-inch wrap cord around it and then let it go over the completed knot.

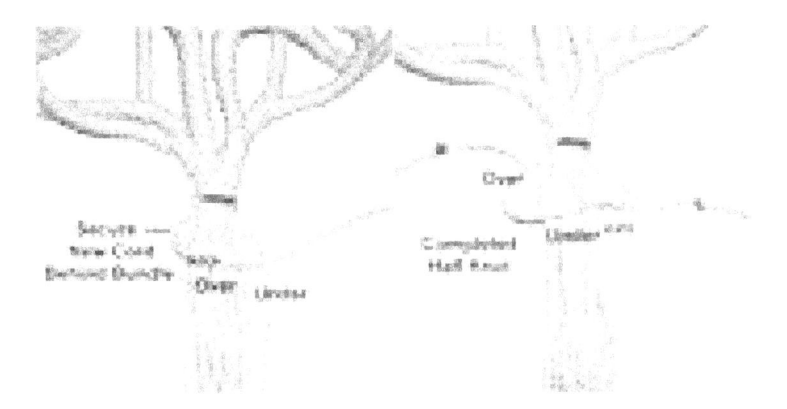

As for the fringe, you have to divide the knots into groups of two and make sure to tie a half-hitch on the rightmost cord on the left, and then let them alternate back and forth continuously under you have managed to cover your whole wreath. Let each sent slide under the whole wreath and then attach each cord to the ring itself.

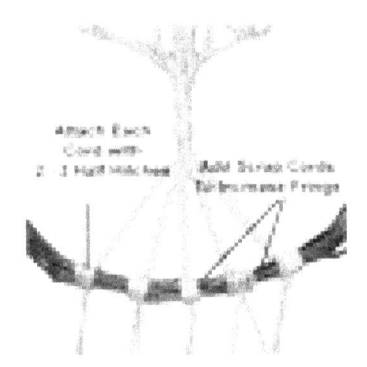

Make sure to divide the cords into small groups and then use the cords so you could tie the overhand knots. Unravel the fibers so you could form a wavy fringe.

That's it! You now have your own Macramé Wreath of Nature!

Conclusion

Taking an ordinary regular room and changing it into a room that will stun guests is the fantasy of most homeowners. The utilization of art, made with macramé hitches, is an extraordinary method to accomplish this fantasy. With such a large number of decisions of artwork finished with macramé ties, there is no uncertainty that you can discover something that coordinates your character and style. Interestingly, every one of these centerpieces is high quality, so they are each one of a kind of creation and makes certain to astonish your visitor whenever they go into your home.

These artworks can be discovered on the internet and can likewise be made by anyone who can tie hitches. Presently I know the greater part of you is considering the macramé that your grandmas used to make. I realize that whenever I consider macramé, the main thing that goes to my head is the plant hangers from the late 70's mid 80's. In any case, the artwork I am talking about is made utilizing materials that include cotton, nylon, hemp, and manila cord. The craftsman making this art utilizes these various materials to wrap bottles and chime ringers and make floor mats, napkins, needle cases, and so forth. With the variety of materials utilized, it isn't elusive things made with macramé knots to arrange with any stylistic theme you have in your home. These artwork pieces would then be able to be set in your home to include some extraordinary touches, particularly any life with a nautical stylistic theme.

It is ideal to have designs that can complement any retire, bar, or wall. Wouldn't a Rum jug secure with macramé hitches look multiple times better sitting on a bar or rack than the regular old, boring container? Envision you pour a beverage for a visitor from a cord secured bottle, at that point give them their beverage to put on a liner made of cord, this after they strolled into your home and cleaned their feet on your floor mat made of the cord also. At long last, a home stylistic layout that is genuinely exceptional, and now the Jones will stay aware of you rather than the reverse way around. What we as a whole need is a room with an excellent point of convergence, and art made with macramé knots will make that point of convergence in any room. All these complicated pieces of art will add a feeling to your space, and individuals will need to know where you got them from, whenever you purchase artwork to brighten your home, recollect that Macramé Knots are not your grandma art any longer.

Macramé can also serve as an avenue for you to begin your dream small business. After perfecting your Macramé skills, you can conveniently sell your items and get paid well for your products, especially if you can perfectly make items like bracelets that people buy a lot. You could even train people and start your own little company that makes bespoke Macramé fashion accessories. The opportunities that Macramé presents are truly endless.

Lightning Source UK Ltd.
Milton Keynes UK
UKHW012111131020
371517UK00014B/160